The Secret of the Mound

Mersea Barrow 1912-2012

Sue Howlett

Published by:

MERSEA ISLAND MUSEUM PUBLICATIONS
HIGH STREET
WEST MERSEA
ESSEX
CO5 8DQ

www.merseamuseum.org.uk

Revised edition, 2013
© 2012 and 2013 Sue Howlett and Mersea Island Museum Trust

ISBN 978-0-9537322-3-4

Printed in England by:

Printwize,
9 Stepfield,
Witham.
Essex
CM8 3BN

www. printwize.co.uk

Contents

Introduction		4
Acknowledgements		5

Part One: The 1912 Excavation
1	Preparing the ground	7
2	Legends of the Barrow	9
3	The excavation begins	11
4	Secrets Revealed	14
5	Details of the excavation	16
6	The tomb and its contents	20
7	A new tourist attraction	24
8	Reporting the Excavation	27
9	Warren's Conclusions:	
	(i) Dating the Barrow	31
	(ii) Cultural significance	32

Part Two: Later History of the Mersea Barrow
1	Sale of the estate	35
2	New ownership	40
3	Enhancing the Barrow	44

Part Three: Interpreting the Mersea Barrow
1	Romans and Britons	49
2	The date of the Mersea Barrow	53
3	Comparative local burials	54
4	Who built the Mersea Barrow?	58
5	Burial rituals	64
6	Further investigation	66
7	Conclusion	73

Bibliography	76
Illustrations and picture credits	79

Introduction

Every Mersea Islander knows the Mersea Barrow, otherwise known as Mersea Mount - or do they? For nearly two thousand years, this ancient mound has guarded the road to East Mersea and the northern shore of the island. It was already more than five hundred years old when the Strood causeway was built by the Anglo-Saxons. Even today, stories cling to the barrow, perhaps the most blood-curdling being the fictional legend, invented by Sabine Baring-Gould in his novel, *Mehalah*, of two Danish invaders, brothers who fought to the death for the love of a captured Saxon maiden. They were buried on either side of the still-living captive, under their upturned boat, 'at the highest point of the island, the great Hoe crowned with black pines'. At every full moon, for all eternity, life would return to the warriors' bones and the clash of their swords could be heard above the weeping of the terrified maiden.

During 2012, Mersea Island Museum celebrated the centenary of the most momentous event in the history of the Mersea Barrow, since it was first constructed by unknown workmen tipping basketfuls of sand and gravel onto the ever-growing mound. On 16th April, 1912, a moustached geologist-archaeologist arrived by train and omnibus to take up temporary residence in the Fairhaven temperance boarding house at West Mersea. His mission was to open a trench into the heart of the Mersea Barrow, and uncover for the first time its long-hidden secrets. Six weeks later, news of his successful excavation aroused public interest and the daily arrival of dozens of eager tourists. Today, a century later, curious visitors are still able to walk gingerly through the same dark tunnel, and enter the eerie candlelit chamber which once concealed a Roman tomb. And the same question is always on everyone's lips: Who built this massive mound, and who was buried within it?

This booklet is divided into three parts. The first retells the story of the first, dramatic excavation of the Mersea Barrow in 1912. The second traces its history during the following, eventful hundred years, during which it was rescued from ignominious service as a glorified chicken run by the Mersea Island Society, which, in 1975, donated the barrow to

Colchester Borough Council. The third part explores new interpretations of this important and impressive funerary monument.

Today the barrow is maintained by the local authority, while Mersea Island Museum Trust provides information and public access to interested residents and visitors. To commemorate the centenary of the 1912 excavation, the contents of the barrow, including the green-glass funeral urn with cremated human remains, were returned to the island where they had lain hidden for nearly two millennia. On temporary loan from Colchester Museum, these items could be seen on display in Mersea Island Museum throughout the summer of 2012. This booklet was first published to accompany the exhibition, telling the story of the excavation and providing further information for anyone seeking answers to the enduring mysteries of the Mersea Barrow.

Acknowledgements

Many people offered help and encouragement in preparing this booklet. When the Mersea Island Museum Trust committee first suggested a commemorative booklet, its two prospective authors visited Colchester Museum's Resource Centre to consult with experts and trawl through the available records. They were helped by Ciara Canning, Curator of Community History, who provided access to dozens of invaluable photographs and documents, including letters written from the excavation site in 1912. Paul Sealey, Curator of Archaeology, produced a pile of relevant background reading and willingly answered questions, even when those answers raised more, unexpected questions!

Inspired by armfuls of photocopies and much new information, the two researchers returned to Mersea to begin their work. Pat Kirby supplied detailed notes and images for this booklet while also preparing audio-visual material and exhibits for the Mersea Museum exhibition, while Sue Howlett continued researching the later history of the barrow and wrote this publication, drawing on the knowledge and resources of experts and local people, most especially those named below.

The chief source for Part One was the detailed report of the 1912 excavation, written by Samuel Hazzledine Warren and digitised by Tony Millatt (who also supplied high quality images from Mersea Museum's digital collection, proved a hawk-eyed proof reader and provided technical assistance in preparing the booklet for publication). Helpful and wide-ranging information on Roman archaeology and burial customs was provided by Ernest Black, who generously allowed use of an early draft of his paper, 'The West Mersea Barrow, Mersea Mount' (2012). A subsequent revised version of this, written jointly by Ernest Black and Stephen Benfield (who provided valuable help dating pottery fragments), is due to be published in *The Transactions of the Essex Society for Archaeology and History*, Volume 4 (Fourth series), 2014 (forthcoming).

As well as offering a ready source of information and support, Colchester and Ipswich Museum Service supplied digital images of rare documents and photographs, with permission to reproduce these. Philip Wise, Heritage Manager, offered help during the revision stages of the first edition of this booklet. Jerry Bowdrey, Colchester Museum's Curator of Natural History, provided information about the ancient seeds collected in 1912 from the soil beneath the Mersea Barrow, while Essex Field Club provided access to their online archives. Other individuals, including members of the Mersea Island Museum Trust, were ready to read, discuss, inform and encourage. Special thanks are due to Roger Wacey of Printwize, for publishing 200 copies of the booklet's first edition free of charge, thus helping Mersea Island Museum to raise funds for analysis of the cremated bone from the Mersea Barrow.

When the human remains from the Mersea Barrow were sent to Salisbury for scientific investigation in early 2013, it was hoped that the sex and age group of the deceased individual might be established. After painstaking analysis, the results proved unexpectedly significant, even unique. The final sections of this revised edition draw on the detailed reports of Jacqueline McKinley, Senior Osteoarchaeologist, Wessex Archaeology, and Rhea Brettell, Archaeological Sciences, University of Bradford. Grateful thanks are due to these two for their meticulous work, and to all who have helped in other ways. All mistakes and omissions, however, remain the author's responsibility.

Part One: The 1912 Excavation

1   **Preparing the ground**

Fig. 1   *Samuel Hazzledine Warren, at home in 1931*

On 16th April, 1912, a sprightly gentleman, resplendent in plus-fours and sporting a bushy walrus moustache, alighted from a Great Eastern steam train at Colchester Station, en route to Mersea Island. His destination was Fairhaven House, still standing today in Seaview Avenue, where he would be staying for most of the next six weeks. The landlady of this temperance boarding house was Mrs Emily Weaver, wife of the local Evangelist Minister, who looked after guests with the help of her eldest daughter, Constance. The gentleman was Samuel Hazzledine Warren, an eminent amateur geologist, who had been commissioned by the recently formed Morant Club to undertake an important investigation on the island.

For centuries, landowners and antiquarians had been fascinated and intrigued by mysterious, ancient remains which dominated the landscape of Britain. While Essex lacked dramatic hill forts or prehistoric stone circles, it could boast several ancient man-made hills - tumuli, or burial mounds - such as the Bartlow Hills on the county's northern border; the Lexden tumulus outside Colchester and the barrow on Mersea Island. Other such burial sites, known to have existed in Essex, had been severely damaged by years of ploughing, gravel-working, or the looting of treasure-seekers.

As the 19th century saw the development of archaeology from a gentleman's hobby to a serious science, archaeological societies sprang up in many English counties. From its foundation as early as 1852, the Essex Archaeological Society began to encourage and report excavations of historic sites throughout the county. In 1880, the Essex Field Club was founded, with Samuel Hazzledine Warren among its members, 'to promote the Study of the Natural History, Geology and Pre-historic Archaeology of the County of Essex and its borderlands'.

In 1909, the short-lived Morant Club was established by a group of professional gentlemen in Essex. Its first chairman was Dr Henry Laver, whose public career included medicine, the mayoralty of Colchester and the honorary curatorship of Colchester Museum. Named after the local historian Philip Morant, the new group described itself as a 'spade club', founded to support the researches of the two existing learned societies by excavating historical sites. The club had a particular interest in the county's mysterious tumuli, particularly since a rich 'princely burial', containing Anglo-Saxon grave-goods including gold and garnet weapon ornamentation, had been discovered in 1888 at Broomfield, near Chelmsford. Following the club's first, disappointing excavation of the Lexden Mount in 1910, one of their next actions was to approach a Mersea farmer, Mr Charles Brown, for permission to excavate the mound in the grounds of his property, Barrow Hill Farm.

The Mersea Barrow, sometimes called Mersea Mount, had been built by hand, unknown centuries before, on one of the highest points of the island, close to an ancient ford across the Pyefleet Channel. In 1912 the mound was measured as 22 feet 6 inches (*6.858 metres*) high with a circumference of about 110 feet (*33.5 metres*), but it had obviously once been considerably larger, and would have provided clear views north towards Abberton, and south towards the River Blackwater and the Roman fort of Othona on the farther shore. There was speculation that it might have been constructed as a beacon hill, giving warning of invasions such as that of the Spanish Armada, but no evidence had been found to support this theory, and it was regarded as more likely to contain an ancient burial.

2 Legends of the Barrow

In common with all ancient remains and desolate places, legends abounded on Mersea Island, focusing particularly on the mysterious barrow. In 1912 these stories ranged from reports of underground passages and secret doors, to terrifying shrieks and sounds of battle heard from the barrow at every full moon. Other ghostly manifestations (still apparently to be seen in the 21st century!) include a Roman centurion pacing over the Strood, visible only from the waist up, often shrouded in mist.

Fig. 2 Warren's photograph of the Mersea Barrow from the west

Before embarking on his excavation, Warren set out to collect evidence of local legends in the hope that these might cast light on the history of the Mersea Barrow. His first approach was to ask the local doctor, Dr Hall, to inquire about them from his elderly patients. He also made note of stories frequently told to him while working on the island, as recorded in his later report:

'There were three women, all desiring to marry the same man, who either fought and killed each other, or else went out to sea in a boat and were drowned. In either case (so said the story), they were all buried together in a boat under the barrow! The details were, however, confused and varied.'

As a practical man of science, Warren was determined to uncover the origin of these tales. While working on his report of the excavation, he wrote to the Reverend Sabine Baring-Gould, former Rector of East Mersea and author of *Mehalah*, the romantic 1881 novel set on Mersea Island. In this novel the sinister villain, Elijah Rebow, tells Mehalah the legend of two Danish invaders, twin brothers who fought for the love of the same captive maiden:

'They fought and smote and hacked one another until their armour was broken and their flesh was cut off, and their blood flowed away, and by nightfall they were both dead. Thereupon the Danes drew up their ship to the top of the hill just above the Strood, and they placed the maid in the hold with a dead brother on either side of her, in his tattered harness, sword in hand, and they heaped a mountain over them and buried them all, the living and the dead together.'

The setting for these gruesome events was named by the author as 'Grim's Hoe' (the devil's barrow), 'at the highest point of the island, the great Hoe crowned with black pines.' The story tells how, at every full moon, the flesh would grow back on the warriors' bones, breath would return to their bodies and they would rise up within the barrow to fight once again, for all eternity, while the terrified maiden looked on.

Warren must have been disappointed by the reply which he soon received from Sabine Baring-Gould. The author confessed that he had no local evidence for this blood-curdling tale but had invented it for dramatic purposes! Although not identical to the legends circulating on the island, there were enough similarities to cast doubt on the stories which Warren had heard. In the end, he was unable to reach a conclusion as to whether these could be traced back to *Mehalah,* or were 'founded upon genuine folk-lore'.

3   The excavation begins

His arrival on 16th April was not Warren's first visit to Mersea. On a preliminary visit, he had consulted with the joint secretaries of the Morant Club, Miller Christy and Francis Reader, as to the best method of opening up the barrow. The club would pay the costs of excavation, amounting to more than £52, so that four workmen could be 'borrowed' from Colchester Corporation to dig into the barrow under Warren's supervision. The intention was to cut a trench, six feet (*1.8 metres*) wide, from the eastern side of the mound into its centre, where they would open up a chamber, twelve feet (*3.6 metres*) square. This was easier said than done. The centre of the barrow proved very difficult to calculate, since its southern and western slopes had been reduced by road building, landscaping and the creation of space for farm buildings. Because of large trees growing on slopes of the mound, the central shaft had to be driven further east then originally intended. Finally, to prevent any dangerous collapse, great quantities of timber had to be brought in to shore up the high sides of the trench and the roof of the central chamber (see fig 11).

Heavy digging continued for the next three weeks, with Warren present on site every day apart from Saturday 20th April, when his place was taken by Mr G. Biddell. On Friday, 26th April, Warren sent a postcard from his lodgings at Fairhaven House to the curator of Colchester Museum, Arthur G Wright, reporting progress to date: 'We are now down eleven feet (*3.3 metres*) from the top in the centre - that is, about half the height of the mound. It has never been opened before...' Prehistoric flints and fragments of pottery had been found, as well as an apparent cooking site, where a mass of charcoal, bone debris and an oyster shell were assumed by Warren to be the remains of a substantial meal which the original builders of the barrow had enjoyed during its construction.

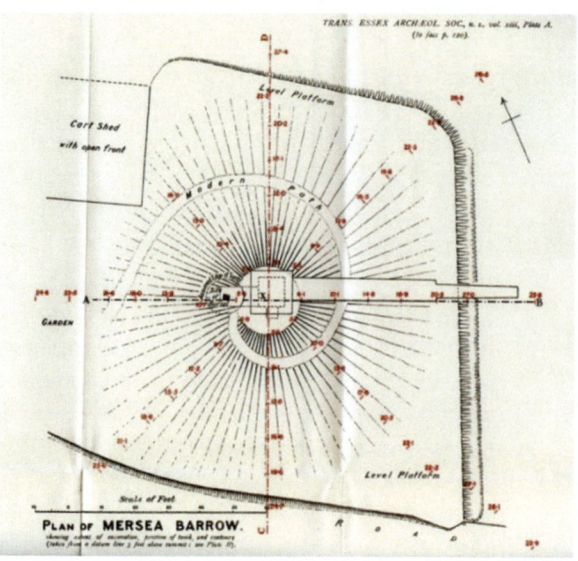

Fig. 3 Warren's plan of the Mersea Barrow

By 8th May, nothing significant had yet been discovered, although the central shaft had been taken down to the original ground level beneath the barrow. Here, many small trial holes were dug below the surface but with no result, leading Warren to conclude that the original builders of the barrow had not dug beneath the ground. Before the excavators could begin searching for the burial chamber at the centre of the mound, Warren was obliged to return to his home at Loughton and all work on the site was suspended until his return on Monday 20th May.

At 11.37 am that morning, Samuel Hazzledine Warren's train pulled into Colchester Station. A few days earlier, he had written to Arthur Wright to arrange a brief meeting at the station, in order to hand over what Warren described as 'casts of the Clacton *Palleolittes*'. These were plaster casts of flint implements and a rare wooden spear-point which he had recently discovered during ground-breaking investigation of the Pleistocene deposits at Clacton-on-Sea, dating from the final glacial periods of the Old Stone Age (see *Essex Naturalist* vol 17, 1912, p.15). He also hoped that the brief eight minutes available, before the bus to Mersea left Colchester at 11.45 am, would allow time for the two men to 'discuss the matters relating to the Mound'! Warren admitted to being so eager to return to his excavation at Mersea Mount that he had no time to spare for calling into Colchester Museum on his way.

His anticipation was rewarded within the next twenty-four hours. Surveying his twelve-foot square shaft near the centre of the barrow, Warren had to decide in which direction to extend the excavation. The west side seemed the most promising, with the exposure there of numerous fragments of Roman roofing tile, charcoal, and a mysterious 'red stratum', which he later described as comprised of crushed red tile and yellow ochre. As the workmen tunnelled their 'heading' for more than four feet (*1.2 metres*) in that direction, more of the same material was found until finally, in the early afternoon of 21st May, their spades struck the solid wall of what could only be a Roman tomb.

Once again, on the cusp of a great discovery, the order was given to stop work, while Warren despatched an urgent telegram from the post office at West Mersea. Addressed to [Arthur] Wright at the Corporation Museum, Colchester, it contained the seven mesmerising words: 'Found small built structure wait opening tomorrow, Warren.' A similar message was sent to Dr Henry Laver, as chairman of the Morant Club who, unlike Wright, was able to come at once to Mersea to witness the opening of the tomb.

Fig.4 Arthur Wright and Dr Henry Laver

The momentous opening of the tomb took place 'in the presence of the chairman [Dr Laver] and many other friends and sympathisers.' As Warren's report continues: 'It was a great day for the inhabitants of Mersea Island, to see the secrets of their barrow, which had for so many generations exercised their wonder and speculation, at last revealed.'

4   Secrets Revealed

And what were the secrets of the barrow? Although readers of Warren's report had to wait a further six pages to read an account of the tomb and its contents, the absent Arthur Wright was soon to receive an excited letter, written from the excavation site on 22nd May. Warren was thrilled to reveal that, peering by candlelight into the chamber at the heart of the mound, he had glimpsed a glass urn containing cremated bone:

> 'My dear Wright,
>
> The 'find' I announced to you by wire has not proved a deception! It is a hollow chamber built of flanged roofing & bonding tiles, perhaps about 2 ft square inside but I have not yet obtained full details. I am anxious not to rush the thing but to get round it carefully. I have worked a candle into the chink we have made in one side, & find that there is a cinerary urn inside, which appears to be perfect. It seems to be contained in a square receptacle which looks like lead, & is covered with two pieces of wood (?) or some other light material.
>
> I think we ought to endeavour to get the structure out, so that it can be preserved in your museum with its contents exactly as it was found. Of course we would break into it in order to get the contents out, but we want to see if anything can be done. Can you come and give us your help?
>
> I am now waiting for timber, as we must get our heading larger before attempting to get it out. Please excuse pencil but I am writing this on the site.
>
> With kind regards,
> Yours sincerely
> S. Hazzledine Warren'

This letter and Wright's reply must have taken only a single day, for on 23rd May Warren was writing from Fairhaven House to sympathise with the family trouble which had prevented Wright from coming to witness the momentous discovery on Mersea. He also thanked Wright for sending cases in which to transport the contents of the tomb to the Colchester Museum for safe-keeping At this stage Warren hoped that the tile-built chamber could be moved and re-erected there, but added, 'I think it might be better to leave it in place until a cart comes to fetch it away. It would need several men with tackle (ropes & pulleys etc) to get it out in as large pieces as possible and then put it together again in Colchester Museum.'

Although one of the tile walls was removed for the tomb to be opened, Warren's hopes that the tomb chamber could be lifted out and reconstructed in the museum proved to be impractical. In September the following year, visitors inside the barrow could still view the opened tile structure, with replicas of the lead box and glass urn now displayed inside. Sadly, all Roman tiles of which the tomb was built have long since disappeared. But the flashlight photograph which Warren took after its opening, together with a cross-section drawing of his conjectural reconstruction (figs 10 and 8), show how the well-concealed burial was revealed to human gaze for the first time in nearly two thousand years.

Resisting the temptation to take the glass urn and cremated bone out of their lead casket, Warren arranged for the complete burial assemblage to be carefully lifted out of the tomb and packed for the journey to Colchester. It was probably fortunate that transport of the fragile glass urn to Colchester Museum did not, as expected, require a horse and cart. Henry Laver's son, Dr Philip Laver, arrived on the scene in time to transport the precious items in his new motor car (described by Warren as a 'dreadful anachronism!').

On arriving at Colchester Castle, the lead casket and glass urn with cremated remains were studied and photographed by the curator, Arthur Wright (fig 5). The Mersea Barrow burial items then became officially part of the Colchester Museum collection, to be admired by generations of visitors over the next hundred years.

Fig. 5 Wright's 1912 photograph of the lead casket and glass urn

5   Details of the excavation

In his formal report, Warren's account of the opening of the tomb is not immediately followed by a description of the burial contained within it, but by a record of the technical details and findings at each stage of the excavation. As workmen extended the trench from the eastern side of the barrow, and the shaft was dug down from the summit, Warren marked out the excavation area with lines of 'latitude' and 'longitude' one foot (*31cm*) apart. He then carefully noted the square in which any fragment of pottery, flint or other specimen was found, with a letter in between two numbers to indicate numbers of feet from the west end; from the northern wall and from the surface of the mound at the point where they were found. Other material found later in the spoil heaps was labelled with 'X' followed by the depth of the layer from which the earth had been dug. These finds were identified in the light of contemporary knowledge and listed in a 'Relic Table' in the 1913 Report.

Fragments of pottery and flint flakes found in the barrow were taken to Colchester Castle to be studied by the curator, Arthur Wright, who contributed a section to the published report. They included three tiny pieces of Roman 'Samian' ware, or *Terrae-sigillata*; 23 of 'Belgic' and 'Upchurch' ware, probably imported from the continent, and 26 of coarse black or red-and-black ware, described as 'British' and probably made locally. There was also a considerable quantity of 'briquetage', fragments of the pottery containers in which sea-water had been boiled to produce salt over many generations in the nearby Red Hills.

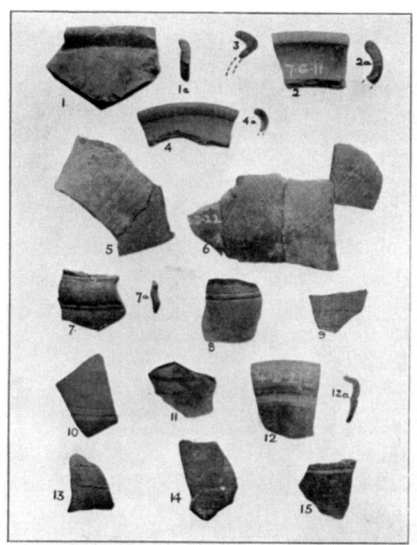 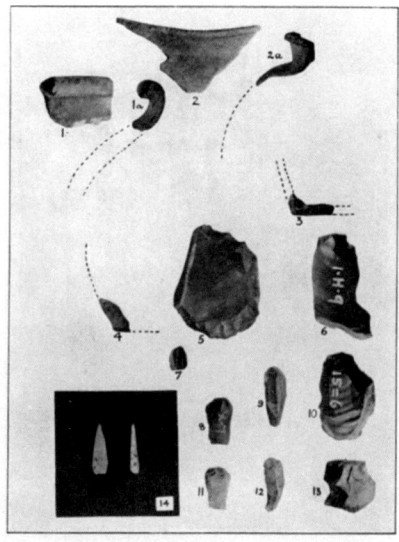

Fig. 6 Warren's photographs of some 'Minor Relics' from the mound

As a geologist, Warren considered carefully the pieces of worked flint discovered during the excavation. These took the form of a few cores and sharp flakes, as well as many waste flint chips, some with a patina of age or calcined by heat, which were found widely scattered throughout the mound. Although he listed the more significant examples in the Relic Table, he considered some of them to be 'no more than accidental', commenting: 'I thought it right to keep everything I found which was in any way suggestive of human workmanship'. He did not believe them to have come from 'any true flint industry', and thought that they had probably 'been gathered up accidentally with the material of which the mound was built'. His final conclusion on the subject of the flints was: 'I found no evidence to indicate contemporary association between the flints and the objects of the age of the barrow' (1913 Report, 135).

In excavating this monument built nearly two millennia earlier, Warren was aware of the need to extract as much information as possible about the environment in which its builders had lived. As he explored the original ground level inside the barrow, he collected a quantity of soil in order to wash out any seeds which would cast light on the flora of the landscape when the barrow was built. Although Warren later professed himself somewhat disappointed with the results produced by their analysis, the collection still survives and is in the possession of the Essex Field Club. (For further information regarding these botanical specimens, see Part 3.6: 'Further Investigation'.)

In the next section of his report, Warren analysed the structure of the mound and the layers of different material of which it was constructed. The lowest layer, up to about twelve feet above ground level, he described as a 'peculiar grey material, which was an impure or earthy quartz sand'. This then gave way to a layer of 'incoherent gravel and sand, with subordinate earthy seams'. Warren concluded that these differing layers had been built up together, since they 'wedged into each other' at the side of the mound with the gravel outside the grey material, and the narrower summit of the mound had then been completed with a layer of gravel. The way in which the layers of gravel and sand at the side of the mound dipped inwards towards the centre suggested to Warren that the gravel had been obtained from the east of the mound and pitched in from that direction. Several thin bands of ironstone had developed between these contrasting layers, and their unbroken state appeared to prove that the mound had never previously been opened. This was exciting evidence that no earlier grave robbers had penetrated the barrow to remove its long-hidden secrets.

One initially insignificant find was described by Warren as 'a piece of decayed wood, an inch and a half or two inches ($c2.5cm$) in thickness, placed perpendicularly above the dome of the tomb.' At the time, he assumed it to be a root, but later discussion with Francis Reader suggested that this might have been the remains of a stake, 'placed there to keep the centre of the mound during the piling up of the earth'.

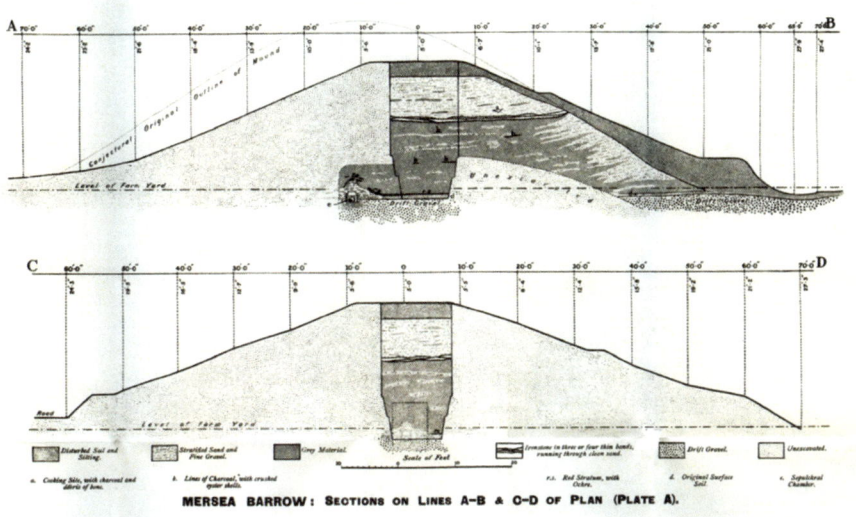

Fig. 7 Warren's cross-section of the barrow

It was clear to Warren, from the way in which the barrow mound had been constructed, that it had 'the stamp of the professional mound-builder, not the novice'. Although its circumference appeared to be pre-planned, there was no evidence of a surrounding ditch. However, the builders appeared to Warren to have left traces of their catering arrangements, for within the grey material comprising much of the barrow, Warren found oyster and mussel shells, fragments of charcoal and, in certain spots, remains of broken shells mixed with charcoal. He attributed these finds to cooking sites and the remains of food eaten during construction of the barrow. A slightly different deposit, measuring 18 inches (*45cm*) by 12 inches (*31cm*) and up to 4 or 5 inches (*c13cm*) deep, which contained charcoal and calcined bone, was also assumed to be a cooking site. Warren sent samples of this burnt bone to a colleague, Mr A C Hinton, who considered most of it to be non-human, although there were some fragments which 'might' have been human but could not at that time be definitely identified as such.

The most mysterious feature which Warren found was what he described as a 'red stratum' (marked as 'r s' on his section drawings). This had been deliberately spread in a layer up to 2 inches (*c5cm*) deep, over the tomb structure and the original ground surface around it, gradually thinning away at a distance of 15 or 20 feet (*c6m*) from the tomb. It was also deposited in several layers of between 1 and 3 inches (*c8cm*) deep, above the 'dome' of the tomb. This red material was made up of crushed red tile and mortar, similar to that used in constructing the tomb, but it also contained yellow ochre, which Warren concluded 'must certainly have been brought there artificially'. In his 1913 Report, the only explanation suggested for the use of the ochre was its possible association with primitive and prehistoric funeral rites, such as those involving the 'Red Lady of Paviland' discovered in 1823, now known to be the skeleton of a young male which had been dyed in red ochre around 33,000 years ago.

Certain features of the Mersea barrow's construction, as observed by Warren in 1912, may indeed have had ritual significance. A century later, these issues continue to be hotly debated in the light of more recent scholarship and archaeological evidence. (See Part 3.5: 'Burial Rituals')

6 The tomb and its contents

Following the exciting moment on 21st May 1912 when the workmen's spades struck something solid, deep within the Mersea barrow, Warren worked patiently to uncover the precise nature of the discovery. As he described in the letter he immediately despatched to Arthur Wright, this proved to be a substantial tomb structure, concealing a hollow chamber which had been constructed to contain the cremation urn inside its lead casket.

The tomb in which the burial was concealed was built entirely of Roman roof tiles (*tegulae*), rising to a dome at the centre, about 22 inches (*55.5cm*) square, and 21 inches (*53cm*) above the roof of the interior chamber. Warren's cross-section diagram of the tomb (Fig 8) shows that below the dome the structure splayed out into two lower layers of increasing size, with a ground-level diameter which he estimated as up to 9 feet (*2.75m*). At its lower, outer limits the tomb was supported by foundations comprising a single layer of stone set in mortar at the original ground level. These boulders were mainly local septaria (fossilised clay) with some flints and a few blocks of imported Kentish ragstone.

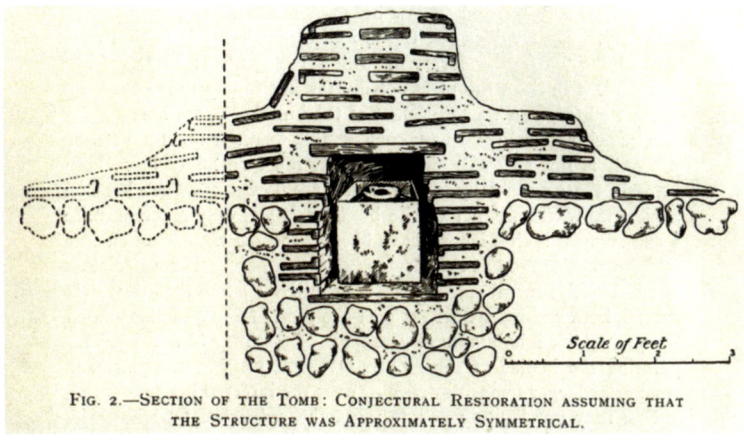

FIG. 2.—SECTION OF THE TOMB: CONJECTURAL RESTORATION ASSUMING THAT THE STRUCTURE WAS APPROXIMATELY SYMMETRICAL.

Fig 8 'Warren's 'Conjectural Restoration' of the tile tomb

Beneath the centre of the tomb, its builders had dug out a pit, probably 3 feet 6 inches (*1.06m*) square and 2 feet 3 inches (*68cm*) deep. This was lined with a double course of the same foundation stone as well as some tiles set in mortar. On this base a floor was formed, 15 inches (*38cm*) below the original ground level, out of two flanged roofing tiles with their flanges (projecting rims) turned downwards. This floor supported the burial chamber containing the cremation urn inside its lead box. Unfortunately, the tomb had been built above what later emerged as a spring of running water, with the result that Warren found that 'both mortar and tiles were in a very soft and decayed state'.

Fig 9 Roman roofing tiles: tegula (flanged) and imbrex (curved)

Within its substantial foundation pit, the lead casket concealing its glass cremation urn nestled snugly at the hollow centre of the tile-built tomb. The walls of this inner, square chamber had been formed as each course of roofing tiles was built up around the edges, with their flanges turned either upwards or downwards, producing a finish which Warren described as 'not more than moderately neat'. The two upper courses overlapped those beneath, supporting a roof to the chamber formed of one single bonding-tile, 21½ inches (*54cm*) square. ('Bonding tiles' were the narrow flat, red bricks which frequently formed a 'bonding' course in Roman walls.)

Tapping carefully with his trowel to open a small chink into the waterlogged chamber, Warren inserted a lighted candle into the cavity. By its flickering light he was able to glimpse the reason why the 'Mersea Mount' had been laboriously constructed, so many centuries before. Through the wavering shadows he could see a box, apparently made of lead, covered with two pieces of what appeared to be wood. He was able to move the makeshift lid sufficiently to see the rim of the glass urn inside. Before any attempt could be made to lift these items out of the tomb, it was necessary to enlarge the 'heading' of the excavation, and Warren ordered more timber so that this could be safely shored up. While waiting on-site for the wood to arrive, Warren took the chance to write his hurried, pencilled letter of 22nd May, asking Wright to come and give advice.

Although Warren had hoped to consult Wright regarding the best way of dismantling the tomb in order to take out the contents, he heard the following day that this had been prevented by a bereavement in Wright's family. So, after shoring up the roof of the excavation, on Thursday 23rd May Warren proceeded to remove the tiles forming one wall of the chamber. As he later reported to Wright, 'I did not touch the structure when I was there, any more than necessary in order to reach the contents. The mortar was very wet & soft but I found that as it became dry it tended to become harder.'

Finally, the opened tomb and its concealed burial were revealed as they had never appeared to the original builders, and would never be seen again. Fortunately, the momentous revelation was recorded by Warren's flashlight camera (Fig 10).

Fig. 10 Warren's flashlight photograph of the opened tomb, with oak covering boards removed.

The lead box, still containing the glass urn, was gently lifted out of its chamber. Although Warren thought it best not to remove the urn, he could see that it was partly filled with fluid, which he attributed to condensation. His prime concern was now to remove these items to safe keeping in Colchester Castle, commenting to Wright, 'I have no doubt that they will be presented to your Museum, but of course I have no authority to present them myself!' His tentative plan to bring the precious items to Colchester himself proved unnecessary when Philip Laver appeared on 24th May in his new motor car, ready to transport the casket and urn to Colchester Castle. Here the urn was at last lifted out of its casket, to be eagerly studied and photographed by Wright (Fig 5). He supplied a detailed description of these items for Warren's 1913 Report:

> 'The bowl, which is globular, is a remarkably fine example of the glass-blower's art and is of unusual size. It is of that cool sea-green hue so much affected by the *Vitrarius* [glass-blower] of Roman times and is transparent. The small mouth is provided with a broad flat ring, sharply turned from a short neck, which adds considerably to the dignity and beauty of the vessel.'

After describing the urn's 'beaded' rim, Wright gave its dimensions which included height of 11 6/16 inches (*29.5cm*) and diameter of 12 14/16

(*31.5cm*). The glass sides were 1/16 inch (*c1mm*) thick, and it stood on a slightly flattened base. Judging, presumably, by the size of the bone fragments, Wright recorded the bowl as containing 'The cremated remains of an adult'.

Rather less beautiful than the glass urn was the functional lead box, which Wright identified as a cist or *ossuarium* (receptacle for the bones of the dead). This was constructed of five plates of lead, cut from a larger sheet, about ¾ inch (*2cm*) thick, and joined together by a blow-pipe without solder. The roughly-square box measured 12 ½ inches (*32cm*) each way and 13 inches (*33.5cm*) deep. In place of a lid, the open top of the box was covered over with two rectangular wooden boards, as Wright commented, 'doubtless to protect the urn from damage during the building-in of the interment'.

7 A new tourist attraction

The removal of the contents of the tomb to Colchester on 25th May 1912 must have left an initial sense of anti-climax, as Warren, the workmen and islanders contemplated the barrow, now opened to the sky, with its empty tomb. The smaller relics, including flints and pottery sherds, had also been sent to Colchester in Warren's personal bag. This must have been promptly returned, since on 30th May, he wrote to Wright: 'Many thanks for returning me the disreputable bag! It has served me on many an expedition for bringing home material for examination.' Warren reported to Wright that he would shortly be meeting Miller Christy and Francis Reader, the joint honorary secretaries of the Morant Club which had funded the excavation. They apparently hoped to persuade him to continue the excavation in the hope of finding further interments within the barrow, although Warren believed that, having found the central tomb with its single cinerary urn, no more significant finds would be discovered by further digging.

Meanwhile, news of the historic finds inside the Mersea Barrow had been given to local newspapers, and intrepid journalists began arriving on the island to cover the story. A report dated 1st June, 1912, told of 'the magnificent glass vase containing the ashes of one of the great ones of a forgotten age, which has been removed to the museum at Colchester this week ...' The anonymous reporter was well briefed, probably by Warren himself, describing the urn's unusual 'entire absence of any iridescence, which is, no doubt, due to the fact of its having been so well protected from the elements all these ages ...' He also commented on 'a faint and yet quite distinct odour of a bituminous character' emanating from the charred bones, possible evidence that some form of bitumen might have been used in the funeral pyre. (It is interesting to note that, while under analysis in 2013, the cremated bones were described as being coated with an unidentified material which gave off 'a noxious choking smell'.)

Within a week, news of the opening of the Mersea Barrow had spread far beyond the shores of the island. Visitors began to appear at Barrow Hill Farm, requesting to see the now famous tumulus and its newly opened burial chamber. Many of these were shown around by Maria Brown, daughter of the farm's owner, who had taken a keen interest throughout the excavation. Thoughtfully, she produced a notebook in which to record the visitors' names, the first being, on Wednesday 29th May 1912, Alexander Kay Barlow, JP, the owner of Wivenhoe Hall. That first open day allowed 37 visitors to enter the Mersea Barrow, including some from London, Suffolk and Surrey. The second day's tally of 50 visitors included three from the far-flung territory of Bongadanga (Bonginda), Upper Congo. These must have been missionaries on leave, since Bonginda boasted the first thatch-roofed missionary church built in that area by 'The Regions Beyond Missionary Union' (Conley, 2009,15) West Mersea's own famous 'fighting parson', Rev. Charles Pierrepont Edwards, made his visit to the excavated barrow on 1st June.

Throughout the remaining months of 1912 Maria Brown was kept busy receiving visitors, eager to see the barrow and to take home a souvenir. On 18th December she wrote to Arthur Wright, asking for more copies of photographs: '(the Mersea Urn) - I will let you know how many dozens we require. I quite imagine visitors to the Barrow will want them - people on the island do, as well as our private friends'. Visitors who came to see the burial chamber walked through Warren's narrow excavation trench, its earth walls towering over 20 feet (*6.1m*) up to the summit of the mound, securely reinforced with timber but still open to the sky. In their prefatory note to the 1913 Report, the joint secretaries of the Morant Club commented: 'As a matter of fact, the excavation remained open for many months after our work was completed. It was, therefore, fortunate that the timbering had been so well constructed.'

Fig. 11
Hammond postcard of 1912-13, showing the open excavation trench

While visitors flocked to visit the excavation, Warren was convinced that nothing could be gained by digging further into the barrow. On 3rd June he wrote to Wright, reporting his decision 'not to go to Mersea any more', provided that Wright could save him 'the time and expense of the journey down' by superintending the removal of the tile structure from inside the barrow. Warren hoped that the tomb could be dismantled in sections and taken to Colchester Castle, concluding his letter, 'I think that the preservation of the structure will immensely increase the scientific value & interest of the contents - this we must discuss further - I am very strong on its preservation.' Warren described how he envisaged the removal of the central part of the tile-built tomb, 'with walls to a thickness of 12 or 18 inches, and the dome over the chamber'. There was no possibility of removing the outlying, lower parts of the stepped tomb, since three of its four sides remained unexcavated. However, Warren hoped that the tomb chamber itself could be reconstructed in Colchester Museum with one side open to display the contents, just as they had been revealed by his excavation. Men, lifting equipment and a cart would be required, but Warren suggested that Mr Goodyear, the Colchester Borough Surveyor who had provided workmen to dig out the trench, would be the best person to provide these.

Warren's letter of 3rd June also provided information about the boxes of other material - 'tiles, septaria etc' - which he had stored in Mr Brown's coal cellar at the neighbouring Barrow Hill Farm. The tiles, which had been carefully removed from the east-south-east wall of the tomb structure when the chamber was opened, had been placed in a separate box and labelled with paper to indicate the different levels of the tile courses, so that they could easily be replaced in a reconstruction of the tomb chamber.

Other material taken from the mound was stored in another packing case, with samples from the mysterious 'Red Band' at the bottom, oyster shells and ironstone above. Warren obviously hoped that this would prove useful for further analysis sometime in the future, and the boxes remained in storage at Colchester Museum. Although an initial search in late 2011 failed to locate them, some of Warren's archaeological samples were rediscovered and studied during the following year. This made possible a revised dating of the pottery sherds preserved and photographed by Warren (Fig 6). (See Part 3.6: 'Further Investigation')

8   Reporting the Excavation

Throughout the summer and early autumn of 1912, Warren was hard at work drafting the manuscript of his report, and working through the pile of archaeological books and reports lent to him by Arthur Wright. Both men were concerned to find out as much as possible about other barrow burials of the Roman period and, in the hope of identifying similar examples, Wright sent a preliminary account of the opening of the barrow to some of the recently formed County Archaeological Societies.

On 2nd October 1912, Wright received a friendly reply from Maud Elizabeth Cunnington of Devizes. This intrepid lady was already well known as an expert amateur archaeologist, who led many ground-breaking excavations including Knap Hill, the West Kennet Long Barrow and Woodhenge, for which she and her husband provided the name. She is said to have spent every winter sorting and identifying pottery, compiling excavation reports and writing articles and books. Her achievements were widely admired, and in 1948 she was the first woman to be made a CBE for services to archaeology (sadly, being ill with Alzheimer's disease, she may never have known of this accolade).

Maud Cunnington had a particular interest in barrows, and was alarmed at the cavalier destruction of many such burial mounds in Wiltshire, 'for such purposes as a golf course near Warminster' (Cunnington, 1912, 603). In her letter to Wright she reported that she had not encountered any burial mounds from the Romano-British period in Wiltshire. However, her extensive knowledge led her to make the perceptive suggestion that the buried individual 'might be someone of Gaulish origin - as late mound burials are apparently so much commoner in some districts of Gaul than they are here?'

By 9th November, 1912, Warren was ready to send an unfinished manuscript of his report to Arthur Wright, for the museum curator to add his contribution. At the same time, Warren returned the borrowed books, which he had found 'most interesting and instructive', with a case of what he called the 'minor relics' for Wright's attention. The intention of the Morant Club, which had financed the excavation, was for the report to appear in the January 1913 issue of *Transactions of the Essex Archaeological Society*. Unsurprisingly, the preliminary work, including washing out the soil samples to extract ancient seeds, had taken considerably more time than expected, while Warren had also been away for much of the summer. His letter provided details of the report's progress and his initial classification of the pottery as listed in his 'Relic Table', which Wright was asked to correct as necessary. Throughout the busy months of this momentous year, Warren's sense of humour remained undiminished: his letter concludes with an apology for 'this long tedious rigmarole' and passes on his wife's concern about 'all our forty-second cousins coming to worry you to see the urn!'

The finalised report, entitled 'The Opening of the Romano-British Barrow on Mersea Island, Essex' was completed in time to appear as planned in the *Transactions of the Essex Archaeological Society* (new series, vol 13, 1913), later published as a separate pamphlet by the Morant Club.

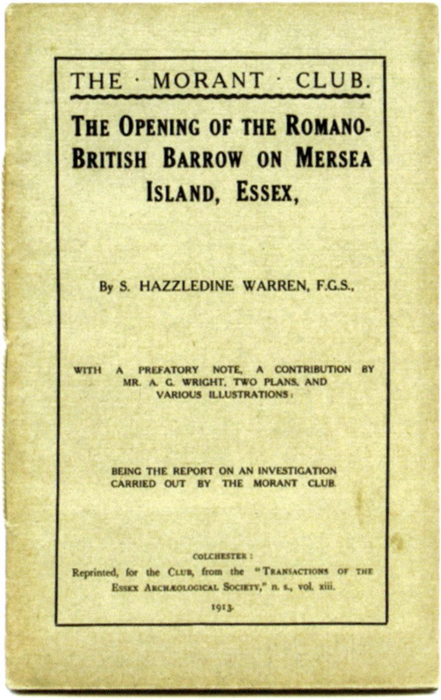
THE · MORANT · CLUB.

THE OPENING OF THE ROMANO-BRITISH BARROW ON MERSEA ISLAND, ESSEX,

By S. HAZZLEDINE WARREN, F.G.S.,

WITH A PREFATORY NOTE, A CONTRIBUTION BY MR. A. G. WRIGHT, TWO PLANS, AND VARIOUS ILLUSTRATIONS:

BEING THE REPORT ON AN INVESTIGATION CARRIED OUT BY THE MORANT CLUB.

COLCHESTER:
Reprinted, for the CLUB, from the "TRANSACTIONS OF THE ESSEX ARCHÆOLOGICAL SOCIETY," n. s., vol. xiii.
1913.

Fig. 12 Cover of the Morant Club reprint of Warren's 1913 Excavation Report

The excavation report began with a 'Prefatory Note' by Miller Christy and Francis W. Reader, the club's joint honorary secretaries, who thanked Mr Charles Brown of Barrow Hill Farm, who, 'like most other inhabitants of the island... keenly desired a solution of the mystery which had so long surrounded the great tumulus'. Their note confirmed that it had proved impossible to remove the brick tomb to Colchester as Warren had hoped, since 'it was found in the end that its large size and exceptionally crumbling condition rendered this a practical impossibility'. Also contained within Warren's extensive excavation report were Wright's contributions on the glass urn and lead cist from inside the tomb, and his identification of the pottery listed by Warren under 'Minor Relics'.

With the publication of his report, Warren had not yet completed his search for a full understanding of every aspect of the barrow. As he informed Arthur Wright on 9th November, 1912, he had spent considerable time 'washing out material & searching for seeds' in the soil samples taken from the mound. The geological and botanical material was then sent to two eminent specialists of Warren's acquaintance. The seeds were sent to Clement Reid, FRS, who had made a special study of fossil seeds (among his many publications was *'Submerged Forests'*, providing early evidence for the submerged land bridge between England and Continental Europe, now known as Doggerland).

On 29th November, 1913, Warren read a paper at a meeting of the Essex Field Club, entitled *'*On certain botanical and geological observations made during the opening of the Romano-British Barrow on Mersea Island*'*. In this, he listed the plant species identified by Clement Reid as having grown on the island at the time the barrow was constructed. Warren obviously found the list unremarkable, commenting 'the results hardly repaid one for the amount of labour that had been bestowed upon the collection.'

Warren then turned to the geological samples which had been sent to G. M. Davies, FGS, of the Imperial Institute, South Kensington. After describing the composition of the ironstone layer and 'grey material', Davies had analysed the mysterious 'Red Stratum' and identified, among the lumps of burnt clay, charcoal and crushed red tile, evidence of yellow ochre. Warren observed that the ochre had been present in greater proportions than appeared from the washed residue. It had then 'clearly been strewn over the tomb after this was closed, the stratum being as much as two inches thick at the centre ...' Warren's only explanation for the strange appearance of yellow ochre was to conclude that it had been part of the funeral ceremony.

Members of the Essex Field Club probably appreciated this additional information about the Mersea Barrow, since many of them had made an excursion to the island, accompanied by Warren, on Saturday 20th September, 1913. They arrived by motor omnibus, alighting to explore the barrow, which they entered 'by a tunnel ... which has been made permanent'. (In the months before their visit, the excavation trench had been roofed over and reinforced with concrete, and the excavated earth replaced above, thus returning the barrow to its original external appearance.) Once in the interior, they were able to observe the tomb chamber 'built up of seven courses of flanged roofing-tiles', inside which were displayed 'carefully-made models' of the original Roman lead casket and glass urn which had been removed to Colchester Museum. It is interesting to note that after visiting a 'red hill' and identifying many plant species and geological features in different parts of the island, the Field Club members visited West Mersea Church and 'the basement of the supposed Pharus [sic], or Roman lighthouse, [which] was an object of very great interest' (later identified as a rare circular mausoleum, or 'wheel tomb'). This was followed by tea in the 'old Tythe Barn' (now Hall Barn).

9   Warren's Conclusions:

(i) Dating the Barrow

It was hoped that by studying the tomb and its contents, as well as pottery fragments found within the mound, the construction of the Mersea Barrow could be approximately dated. In a section which he contributed to Warren's 1913 excavation report (pp130-3), Arthur Wright carefully compared these artefacts with similar examples of Roman cremation burials and the objects associated with them. The beautiful glass urn bore a close resemblance to three others found in Colchester and now in the Castle Museum, two of which also held cremated remains, the smaller one containing 'the burnt remains of a child and its pet bird', accompanied by two small jars which might originally have contained food for the child and the bird. These attractively decorated beakers were identified as coming from the Roman potteries at *Durobrivae* (near Castor, Cambridgeshire) and dating from the early 2nd century or perhaps, as Wright suggested from other evidence, the late 1st century.

Among other examples of early Roman burials, Wright described those found at Warwick Square, London, in 1881, which bore several similarities to the Mersea Barrow burial. At the London site, a glass cremation vessel was found inside a cylindrical container, made of a sheet of lead which had been rolled and the sides joined by a blow-pipe without the use of solder. This was the same process that had been used to join the cut sheets of lead forming the casket which contained the Mersea cremation urn. (Now known as the 'burnt joint process', this method of sealing lead joints was not re-discovered until the first half of the 19th century.) Since a second burial on the same site included a coin of the

Emperor Claudius, the Warwick Square cemetery appeared to date from the second half of the 1st century AD.

Fragments of pottery found in the barrow were taken to Colchester Museum to be studied by Wright. Warren had already divided the potsherds into separate groups, as listed in his 'Relic Table' and photographed (Fig 6). The pieces were generally too small to provide a clear idea of the shape of the broken vessels; this was especially unfortunate in the case of three tiny fragments of *Terra-sigillata* or 'Samian' ware, since this fine table-ware, widely imported from Gaul, often bore rich relief decoration and the stamp of the potter who had made it. These pieces were dated by Wright to the 1st century AD. The most numerous types of pottery were described as 'Belgic and Upchurch wares', both originating from the continent and produced in colours ranging from black and grey to red or brown. The second most numerous group was that of coarse black ware, which Wright described as common during Late Celtic and Roman times for cooking purposes, and probably of local manufacture.

Basing his conclusions on examples known to archaeologists of the early 20th century, Wright suggested a date for the Mersea Barrow as falling within the period of the Flavian emperors, Vespasian, Titus and Domitian, who ruled Rome between AD 69 and 96. This would have been only a short time after the revolt of the Iceni tribe led by Boudica, who sacked Colchester in AD 60. Warren was happy to accept this suggestion, concluding his report, 'It appears we may fix the date of the interment to the latter half of the first century AD'. (See Part 3.6 'Further Investigation' for recent reconsideration of this evidence.)

(ii) Cultural significance

In the concluding section of his 1913 Report, Warren reflected not only on the age of the Mersea Barrow but on the cultural significance of this form of burial, under an earthen mound, or tumulus, which had probably once been considerably higher than the 22 feet 6 inches (*6.8m*) surveyed in 1912. He was aware that the use of tumuli in Britain 'went out of use with the Early Bronze Age, and re-appeared with the advent of Roman influence in this country', which struck him as puzzling, 'when we consider that barrow-building was not a Roman custom'. He was more inclined to attribute the Mersea Barrow, and other mounds from the same period, to 'Belgic or Scandinavian influence' ... 'a fair indication of a non-Roman race, although it may have been living under Roman influence'.

As a regular reader of *Transactions of the Essex Archaeological Society*, Warren would have been very interested in an article, which appeared in 1899, on the Bartlow Hills (formerly in north Essex but now transposed into Cambridgeshire). There were originally eight of these round Roman tumuli of which only three are clearly visible today, the largest 40ft (*12.2m*) high and 145ft (*44m*) in diameter. The author, A R Goddard, described the opening of the barrows during the 1830s, and the spectacular finds contained within them. These included 'a glass bottle ... which was two-thirds full of a yellow fluid, covering a deposit of human bones' and 'the cremated bone deposit in a green glass bottle...'

Fig. 13 The Bartlow Hills, as seen in a print of 1780

Unlike the Mersea Barrow, at Bartlow many fine grave-goods had been deposited with the human remains, among them a folding stool; 'a graceful pitcher with ornament in silver inlay; a bronze lamp with richly wrought acanthus leaf for handle; a unique little incense pot of bronze, with design in overlay of red, blue, and green enamel.' Unfortunately, most of the finds were destroyed in a great fire at Easton Lodge, although drawings of them survive and, in 1899, the blackened remains of the enamelled urn could be seen in the British Museum

In the final paragraphs of his 1913 Report, Warren quoted the view of A R Goddard that the Bartlow Hills were 'essentially non-Roman, although erected by the Romanised Britons and during the Roman occupation of this country'. Goddard, in line with many historians of his day, believed that, 'Barrow making ... was not a Roman introduction. It belonged to the people already by long centuries of usage ... If these mounds were really erected in memory of some prominent Roman, his friends were not following the custom of their own land, nor of their own times, but the practice of the people among whom they had settled.' Additional evidence for this view was apparently provided by the lack of any inscription identifying the deceased, such as those often found with Roman burials.

Encouraged by this scholarly interpretation of a nearby barrow cemetery from the early Roman period, Warren concluded his report on the Mersea Barrow in similar vein:

> 'Tumuli entailing labour of such magnitude, like the Bartlow Hills or the Mersea Mount, would only be erected for persons of great importance. It seems to me in the highest degree improbable that an important personage of a more highly cultured race would be buried according to the custom of a more barbarous people whom they had conquered. On the other hand, it appears exceedingly probable that the tomb of a petty ruler of the more barbarous race would betray the influence of the more cultured race under whose suzerainty he held his office.
>
> 'Thus, although we have unfortunately no clue to the name, I think that we may reasonably suppose Mersea Mount to be the tomb of some important personage or petty ruler of British race, but living under Roman influence.'

Despite its stereotypes of the British tribes as 'barbarous', this Edwardian view of the cultural context of the Mersea Barrow has remained widely accepted and rarely questioned until the later decades of the 20th century. Indeed, the hypothetical scenario of an intermarriage between a chieftain of the Trinovantes (or his daughter) and a Roman incomer has an enduring, romantic appeal. Generations of islanders could easily imagine the grief of a Roman official, laying his British bride to rest in a fine Roman glass cremation urn, within a burial mound built by her native family according to their ancient tradition. The nearby tumulus at Lexden, west of Colchester, might appear to support such an interpretation, since it probably commemorates the British ruler Addedomaros, buried with a medallion of the Emperor Augustus, within a mound now only around 5 feet (*1.5m*) high. However, such clear-cut explanations for the origin of the Mersea Barrow can no longer circulate unchallenged, and are discussed in Part Three: 'Interpreting the Mersea Barrow'.

Part Two: Later History of the Mersea Barrow

1   Sale of the estate

In the summer of 1912, when the newly excavated Mersea Barrow swarmed with daily troops of visitors, life for the occupants of Barrow Hill Farm must have seemed very different from the regular routines of their former life. The owner, Charles Brown, had bought the farm in 1902, moving from Edmonton, Middlesex, where the 1901 census listed him as a brickmaker and employer. His wife died in 1908, and three years later he was listed as 'Brick-merchant and Builder', living at Barrow Hill Farm with his 79 year-old sister-in-law, Rebecca Day, and his unmarried daughter, Maria Brown. Maria was a former schoolmistress of 36 who, following the marriage of her only sister in 1903, had given up her profession to care for her elderly father and aunt with the help of a live-in servant, Ivy Packer, aged 18. For a few exciting months in 1912 and on many occasions afterwards, Maria was kept busy greeting visitors, showing them inside the barrow and offering souvenir postcards of the Roman casket and urn.

Fig. 14 Early postcard of Barrow Hall (Barrow Hill Farm)

On the outbreak of war in 1914, Maria and her elderly father still lived at Barrow Hill, although visitors were probably less frequent by now. The large Victorian farmhouse with very few neighbours must have felt remote from the community and amenities of West Mersea, and by the end of the war it seems that they had moved to a more convenient house, 'Averham', in Seaview Avenue. Kelly's Directories for the post war years show that Charles Brown was living there until 1922, the year in which he died, aged 93, leaving an estate of £10,085 (*England and Wales National Probate Calendar*). Maria Bown continued as sole householder of Averham until 1925, but by 1936 the house had a new occcupant, listed on the Electoral Register of that year as Rebecca Amelia Frost.

Barrow Hill Farm, meanwhile, had been taken over by Mr A E Cook, who in the 1925 *Kelly's Directory* is listed as a farmer of over 150 acres. However, it seems that Mr Cook was more interested in property development than in agriculture, being fully aware that his land included valuable frontage of 1460 feet (*445 metres*) along the main road to East Mersea. In 1929 the Barrow Hill Estate totalling about 152 acres was put on the market in several lots, to be sold by auction at a 'low reserve' price, at the Colchester Corn Exchange Board Room, on Saturday 6th July, 1929. In the agent's introductory remarks, no mention was made of the farm's agricultural productivity; instead, the potential buyer was informed that,

'The land lends itself readily to development as a building estate, and is close to the rapidly rising seaside resort of East Mersea with its new 18 hole Golf Course and Club House.' Another page of the sale particulars reiterated hopefully, in bold print, 'It is suitable for Development as a Building Estate.'

The farmhouse offered for sale was described as a 'Comfortable, Old-Fashioned Residence', with five bedrooms over three floors, although its single bathroom was supplied only with cold water from the outside pump and well. Around half of the attached farmland was saltmarsh and the many outbuildings included a licensed slaughter house. There were two tenanted farm cottages and a 'Pretty, Detached Bungalow' with the intriguing, Hindustani name of 'Chota Kamra' (small room). In small print under the farm details occurred an incidental note: 'Adjoining the Farm Premises is an ancient Barrow or Tumulus, which is registered at Whitehall as a national antiquity'. The Barrow, otherwise known as Mersea Mount, had been first scheduled as an Ancient Monument in 1923 and thus officially protected from destruction, although its surroundings would have been radically changed if the advertised 'building estate' had ever been developed!

*Fig. 15
1929 Sale Map of the Barrow Hill Estate, showing the Mersea Barrow in the bottom right corner.*

Fortunately, Mr Cook's ambitious hopes for a lucrative building development close to the Mersea Barrow were as ill-fated as East Mersea's future as a 'rising seaside resort'. Instead, the new farmer of Barrow Hill was listed in the 1933 Kelly's Directory as Olaf de Manby, although the farmland had now shrunk to below 150 acres, with the separate sale of the smaller lots. In 1936 his full name was recorded on the Register of Electors, as 'Aban' Olaf Henry de Manby, Barrow Hill Farm.

The impressive name of the new owner of Barrow Hill can be traced back to a family entitled to its own coat of arms (Fox Davies 1929, 1300). Born in 1881, Alban Henley Olaf Manbey, who adopted the name of de Manbey by deed poll, was the son of the vicar of St Alban's, Acton, Middlesex. In 1906 he married Catherine Ward of Winterdale Manor, Althorne, Essex, where they lived until 1929. In 1915 their only son was born, given the confusingly similar name of Alban Gerald Olaf Manbey. Meanwhile, Alban Henley Olaf Manbey enlisted in the Royal Field Artillery, serving with distinction in France during the Great War

In November 1916, 'Temporary 2nd Lt Alban Manbey' was recommended for the Military Cross. The citation cited his 'conspicuous gallantry. With the assistance of two men he dug out six men of another unit, who had been buried in a dug-out, and got them into safety. He was working over an hour under intense shell fire' (11060 *Supplement to the London Gazette* 14th Nov 1916). By 1917 he was promoted to the rank of Captain and following further military service became Major Manbey.

After the war, Major Manbey returned to his wife's family home at Althorne, remaining there until his purchase of Barrow Hill Farm in 1929 brought the family to Mersea. Catherine de Manbey died in 1936, and within a few years her widower leased Barrow Hill Farm to tenants, moving to a house named 'Pantiles' in Victory Road. During the Second World War, he is remembered by local residents as having served with the Home Guard.

On 10th June, 1943, at West Mersea church, Alban Henley Olaf de Manbey, described as 'MC, Officer [Retired], Widower,' was married to Marjorie Chambers, whose deceased father had been a colliery owner. The address for both was given as 'Pantiles', Victory Road, West Mersea. Here they continued to live, having no children of their own but adopting a daughter. In the summer of 1951, Major Manbey died at the age of seventy. Strangely, the telephone directory for 1958 shows 'Major A H O Manbey' still listed at 'Pantiles', Victory Road, probably because his widow left the entry unchanged.

Although Mrs Marjorie Manbey no longer lived at Barrow Hill, she still owned the ancient barrow which Warren had excavated in 1912. During the 1950s, local people wishing to enter and view the burial chamber were able to call at Barrow Hill Farm and borrow the key from members of the Frost family who were then living there. However, the condition of the monument was causing concern, which spread beyond local boundaries to become the subject of a question in Parliament. As recorded in *Hansard* for 24th June, 1958, Anthony Greenwood, MP for Rossendale and later a Labour minister and peer, asked the Minister of Works: 'What steps he is taking to prevent further damage by trees and animals to the tumulus on Barrow Hill, West Mersea?'

This must have seemed a surprising choice of question for a Lancashire MP, but Anthony Greenwood knew Mersea well since his father, the Rt Hon Arthur Greenwood, had lived at the Old Ship Cottage, East Mersea for much of the war, even during the time when he was a member of the Churchill's War Cabinet. Anthony Greenwood stood as prospective Labour party candidate for Colchester before the war and continued to spend time at the family home at East Mersea, loving the island so much that when he became a member of the House of Lords in 1970, he took the title 'Baron Greenwood of Rossendale, of East Mersea in the County of Essex' (information from Susanna Taylor née Greenwood). Responding to his questioner's challenge regarding the poor condition of the Mersea Barrow, Hugh Molson, the Essex-born Conservative minister, gave his typical reply: 'I am looking into this and will write to the hon. Member.'

Any letter which the Minister of Works might have written did nothing to improve the state of the Mersea Barrow. In an article for *Essex Countryside* in 1969, Leslie Haines (subsequently one of the founding members of Mersea Island Museum) described the conditions that had prevailed since the war:

'The Mersea Island barrow has for the last twenty-odd years been the home of chickens from the farm next door. Through the effects of weather, the activities of the chickens and the general neglect, the barrow slowly disappeared from the public's view under scrub hedges, brambles, old car bodies and farm machinery. Dug into the side of the mound is a derelict cart shed, most of the tin roof rusted and fallen away.'

Fig. 16 Mersea Barrow, grazed by chickens, in 1966

2   New ownership

Although the Mersea Barrow was a listed Ancient Monument, the Ministry of Public Buildings and Works showed no interest in maintaining it, and the National Trust, also approached by the Mersea Island Society in 1966, was unable to take it on. Fortunately, a solution was at hand. Perhaps tempted by the relief of shedding responsibility for the barrow, its owner, Mrs Manbey, generously donated the Mersea Barrow to the Mersea Island Society. The Society appointed four trustees, who immediately launched an appeal to raise funds for the barrow's restoration, and to make it accessible to visitors. By the end of 1966, about £200 had been raised, sufficient to remove the chicken houses and cut down undergrowth and smaller trees. A bulldozer was brought in to reconstruct the contour of the barrow as nearly as possible to the original shape. Then iron railings and a wooden gate were erected, with a small bay left in which to park cars. The following year, about 400 spring bulbs were planted to enhance the appearance of the barrow. All these improvements earned a commendation from the Civic Trust in 1968.

Despite the early success in fundraising, the costs of maintaining the barrow placed a considerable strain on the resources of the Mersea Island Society. Attempts were made to pass on responsibility for the Mersea Barrow to the local authority, but in July 1970 Essex County Council declined to take this on, although they offered to contribute £25 per annum towards its upkeep. West Mersea Urban District Council agreed in 1972 to donate £315 per annum, as well as paying for expert pruning of trees on the barrow.

Fig. 17 Mersea Barrow in 1969, following clearance and renovation

Finally, in 1974, two years after the death of Mrs Manbey, the Mersea Island Society resolved to approach Colchester Borough Council in order to 'present' it with the ownership of the barrow. Dr Alec Grant, Secretary to the Trustees of the Mersea Barrow, wrote to the Chairman of Colchester's Cultural Activities Council on 11th June, 1974. After giving a full account of the barrow's history and the society's work to restore and maintain it, his letter concluded:

> 'In view of the unique character of this ancient monument and the interest shown by the public and particularly the educational value to schools, the Trustees feel the ownership should be vested in a permanent authority such as yours, rather than the ephemeral existence of such bodies as trustees or an amenity society.
> We therefore wish to offer to present the ownership of the Mersea Barrow to the Borough of Colchester'.

This was an offer that Colchester Borough Council felt it could not refuse, and the official transfer of ownership of the Mersea Barrow took place on 16th April, 1975. Leslie Haines, Chairman of the Trustees, handed over the deeds of the barrow to the Mayor of Colchester, Councillor James Jackson.

Fig. 18 The handover of the Mersea Barrow to Colchester Borough Council

Sometime during 1975, BBC television viewers were able to see the ancient Mersea Barrow, filmed for an episode of 'On Camera' which featured scenic locations, traditional skills and eloquent residents of Mersea Island. (This programme can still be viewed, courtesy of the East Anglian Film Archive, on *http://www.eafa.org.uk/catalogue/4832*). In the foreground of a fine view of the barrow, a notice could be seen informing the public that the monument was in the care of the Mersea Island Society and that a key could be obtained from Major R Johnson, who lived at the nearby 'Bower Haven' on East Mersea Road. Visitors borrowing the key would be asked to sign the Mersea Barrow Visitors' Book. Interviewed at the site, Major Alan Mansfield, a local historian and amateur archaeologist, described the barrow as a Romano-British burial mound which had probably contained the burial of a Celtic chieftain. TV viewers were even able to see film footage of the barrow's interior with its empty chamber, from which the tile-built tomb, observed there by visitors in 1913, had been removed by persons unknown during the previous six decades.

As the new owners of Mersea Barrow, Colchester Borough Council undertook its regular maintenance, preserving the ancient monument as an attractive, mysterious destination for visitors. During 1975, elm trees were removed from the barrow and the topsoil restored and seeded. Although the burial chamber within the barrow was now empty, the lead casket and glass urn found within it could be seen on display in Colchester Castle Museum. When the newly established Mersea Island Museum opened its doors in 1976, the Museum Trust also became key-holders for the barrow, arranging escorted visits for anyone who wished to enter the burial chamber or walk over the mound. Since that time, generations of local people, visitors and school parties have been able to book a free guided tour of the barrow. Over nearly four decades, enthusiastic committee members have given a vivid account of the barrow's history and hidden secrets to many hundreds of curious visitors.

With the coming of the new millennium, an increasing interest in local history brought frequent comments about the lack of public awareness of the Mersea Barrow. Although visible from the road, the barrow could easily be missed by passengers speeding by in a car, unaware of its existence. With limited space for car parking and no information panels to explain its historic significance, the site failed to appear on any 'Heritage Tourist Trail'. (Interestingly, it has appeared on databases of paranormal sightings. Sabine Baring-Gould's fictional legend of 'Grim's Hoe' qualifies Mersea Barrow to feature on the list of 'Top Ten Haunted Sites', drawn up by Jennifer Westwood and Jacqueline Simpson for the *Independent* newspaper of 11th July 2008.)

3 Enhancing the Barrow

When compared with Colchester's own rich Roman heritage, Mersea Island might seem a historic backwater. However, the 'list entry summary' on English Heritage's database of Ancient Monuments points out the rarity and significance of what is there named as 'Mersea Mount' (list entry number 1019019):

> 'The survival of Roman barrows as upstanding earthworks is rare nationally and extremely rare in East Anglia. The use of a barrow at West Mersea to demarcate a cremation burial is not unique in Roman Britain, however, Mersea Mount is unusual in that Roman barrow burials are usually found in groups (such as the Bartlow mounds at Ashdon). This lone, large barrow is indicative of a very high status burial ...'

With all this in mind, in December 2001 Colchester Borough Council was reported to be preparing to submit a bid for £20,000 of lottery funding to bring the Mersea Barrow 'back to the future and to the attention of the public'. If successful, the project would improve access to the site, install electric lighting along the entry passage and erect information boards telling the history of the barrow. Sadly, the lottery bid came to nothing, but the plans remained as aspirations which might be achieved if future funding became available.

Since the sale and break-up of the Barrow Hill estate in 1929, land to the east of Mersea Barrow had been farmed separately. During the 1950s it was farmed by Jack Marriage, a well-known Mersea farmer. The only building close to the eastern side of Mersea Barrow was Barrow Farm Barn, shown on maps dating from 1838. In 1997 and 1998, planning applications were made for change of use of the now redundant barn from agricultural to business use. In the light of the rural location and adjacent ancient monument, these applications were refused. However, when Mr and Mrs Roger Wacey acquired the land with its dilapidated barn, new and more imaginative plans were put forward.

In 2003, the first of a series of planning applications was submitted to Colchester Borough Council, proposing that Barrow Farm Barn be converted to a dwelling. This would be accompanied by the provision of public parking with access to the adjacent ancient monument, ie the Mersea Barrow. Unsurprisingly, this proposal was welcomed by Colchester Museums whose then Curator of Archaeology, Philip Wise, wrote on 6th June 2003:

> 'In my judgement the present proposal represents the best chance for Colchester Borough Council Leisure Services to realise its objectives in relation to Mersea Mount. This is a very rare opportunity to increase public access and improve the setting and interpretation of the monument. Such opportunities may only occur once in a generation.'

The application was also supported by West Mersea Town Council and, significantly, by Deborah Priddy, Inspector of Ancient Monuments for English Heritage Eastern Region. She wrote to Colchester's Planning Officer on 29th July 2003:

> 'I do not feel that there will be any adverse impact on the setting of the monument: indeed, there would clearly be benefits in terms enhancing the interpretation and visitor amenity of the scheduled monument. Providing the conversion of this barn does not conflict with your plan policies regarding the conversion of agricultural buildings, we would welcome the enhancement of the monument which these proposals would bring.'

Despite such widespread support, this application was officially refused on 13th August 2003, on the grounds that: 'The site lies within the Rural Area, defined as a Countryside Conservation Area ... While the proposal includes improving access to a Scheduled Ancient Monument, this does not outweigh the local plan policies for housing in the countryside.'

A welcome opportunity to improve Mersea Barrow's attraction and accessibility to visitors was thus significantly delayed. The rejected application was followed three years later by a new proposal, accompanied by an Information Statement brochure dated August 2006 which, with the use of old maps, background history and colourful photographs, put forward a series of persuasive arguments. The converted building would be integrated into the Countryside Conservation Area 'by use of sustainable technologies combined with improvements to landscape and wildlife habitats'. Any doubts which Colchester Borough Council may have had regarding legal ownership would be allayed by a 'legal agreement giving the Borough Council control over the new access and parking areas as well as alterations to the barn site and buildings that could affect the setting of the historic monument.' Once again, this application was supported by the Colchester Museums and by English Heritage, who wrote of the plans: 'They offer the borough council the opportunity to ensure the long-term maintenance of the monument and, equally importantly, provide low-key facilities such as parking, viewing space and interpretation.'

Despite the continuing doubts of Colchester's planning officers, who recommended refusal, the application was conditionally approved in September 2006. This permission was renewed with an extended time limit on 1st December 2011, and at last it appeared that the opportunity had arrived to 'turn an eyesore into an asset, to sympathetically enhance the location and make the barrow a safe attraction for the people of the borough and visitors to Mersea' (R Wacey, quoted in *Essex County Standard*, 29th September 2006).

In the early months of 2012, the year which brought the centenary of the excavation of Mersea Barrow, significant changes were taking place. On Friday, 17th February, a group of eager visitors, wishing to see inside the burial chamber, were greeted by the sight of cheery workmen preparing the site for the improved vehicle access and parking (fig 19). By the end of the year a wide entrance road, several parking bays and a turning area had been provided by Mr Wacey for visitors to the Mersea Barrow. This allowed a great increase in visitors, culminating in the Heritage Open Weekend of September 2012. In those two days, more than a hundred visitors, many of whom had already seen the display in Mersea Museum, were able to enter the barrow and learn more about Mersea Island's rare and impressive Roman burial mound.

*Fig. 19
Visitors to the Mersea Barrow, on 17 February, 2012. The old barn and evidence of new landscape work can be seen in the background.*

The century since the Mersea Barrow was excavated in the spring of 1912 has brought many changes both to the island and to the condition and surroundings of the ancient tumulus. The original excavation report, with its many plans and photographs, revealed for the first time exactly what was concealed within the conspicuous earthwork, which must have taken so many man-hours to construct. However, many questions remained regarding the identity of its builders and its clearly important occupant.

In 1912, Samuel Hazzledine Warren carried out what has since been described as an 'exemplary' archaeological excavation of the Mersea Barrow. He arranged for his carefully garnered collection of archaeological, geological and botanical specimens to be sent to the appropriate museums for safe storage and possible future analysis. As noted in the English Heritage List Entry Summary, the barrow had been only partly excavated and much was still to be discovered:

> 'Artefacts and environmental evidence will have survived and may, through the use of modern scientific analysis, add to our knowledge of the construction and appearance of the barrow and of Roman Mersea at the time of the mound's construction.'

Perhaps, at last, 'modern scientific analysis' might begin to reveal more about the construction and significance of the Mersea Barrow.

On 23rd April 2012, the centenary celebration of Mersea Barrow's excavation began amid much excitement. A Colchester Museum Service van drew up outside Mersea Museum, and soon its precious freight was carried inside by Steve Yates and two assistants. The lead casket, glass urn and cremated remains of a deceased Roman had returned to the island where they had been buried nearly two millennia before. The items were placed on the floor to await assembly of a massive glass display case, in which they were then carefully placed on suspended glass shelves. The case was securely locked, the key taken away and museum volunteers left with a week in which to complete the display, of which the bones in their ancient containers would be the striking centrepiece.

Fig. 20
Colchester Museum staff moving the Roman cremation urn into its temporary display cabinet in Mersea Museum

23rd April, 2012

Mersea Museum's 2012 exhibition, 'Buried Secrets', proved a huge success. Hundreds of individuals, schoolchildren and other groups, from the island and further afield, visited the museum display. Many also ventured inside the Mersea Barrow, and large numbers donated to the appeal to raise funds for bones from the barrow to be analysed. By the end of the year, more than £1000 had been contributed by the public, and this sum was more than doubled by generous donations from the Mersea Island Society and the Association for Roman Archaeology. Once permission was obtained from Colchester Museum Service, plans were made for the long-awaited analysis of the ancient cremated bone to go ahead.

Part Three: Interpreting the Mersea Barrow

1   Romans and Britons

Following the excavation of 'Mersea Mount' by Samuel Hazzledine Warren for the Morant Club in 1912, the published report was given the title *The Opening of the Romano-British Barrow on Mersea Island, Essex.* This early description of the barrow as 'Romano-British' gained acceptance, appearing to explain the apparent discrepancy of a Roman burial within a 'non-Roman' burial mound, or tumulus. Both Warren and Arthur Wright believed that 'barrow-building was not a Roman custom', and this prevailing view was succinctly summed up in 1969 by one of the then trustees of the barrow: 'Romans did not build barrows, and the Britons did not put their dead into Roman bottles and caskets' (Haines, 1969, 633).

Whether the barrow was built by Britons, Romans, a Romanised British population or even two co-operating communities is a complex question, since these terms are often used to convey a wide range of definitions. One early, romantic view of the 'Romano-British' character of the Mersea Barrow attributed its construction to the burial of a British woman married to a Roman, yet the same term might now be applied to any feature of Britain under Roman rule. 'Roman' often implied holding Roman citizenship, a privileged status granted only after AD 212 to all free men in the Roman Empire. However a wealthy Romanised Briton before that date might describe himself as Roman, while even freed slaves or retired soldiers from anywhere in the empire could be granted Roman citizenship.

The approximate age of the Mersea Barrow is also significant in assessing its cultural background. In his report, Warren accepted the conclusion of Arthur Wright, the Curator of the Colchester Castle Museum and a respected officer of the Essex Archaeological Society, that the glass bowl which contained the cremated remains could be dated to the period of the Flavian emperors, between AD 69 and 96. This late 1st century dating appeared to be confirmed by the pottery fragments found in the barrow, as listed and described by Wright (1913 Report 135-7). If this dating were correct, the barrow would have been constructed within a generation of the revolt of Boudica, queen of the British Iceni tribe, and the total destruction of the Roman provincial capital, Colchester, only nine miles from Mersea.

Roman Colchester, or *Colonia Claudia Victricensis,* occupied the site of the earlier legionary fortress established within the British 'oppidum' (major settlement) of Camulodunum. The local population were Trinovantes, who with their western neighbours, the Catuvellauni, were ruled over for many years before the Roman invasion by Cunobelin, probably from Camulodunum where much of his coinage was minted. Archaeology in this area has revealed cultural and trading links with the Roman Empire as well as with the Belgic tribes of northern Gaul, now part of the Roman world. So great was the power and prestige of Cunobelin that the Roman writer, Suetonius, described him as 'King of the Britons'.

When Cunobelin died in *c* AD 40, internecine conflict had already brought appeals for intervention from Rome. These came at an ideal time for the insecure new Roman emperor, Claudius. If he could claim the conquest of Britain, which even the mighty Julius Caesar had failed to achieve in 55-54 BC, his position would be assured. In AD 43 the Roman commander Aulus Plautius led his legions out of Kent towards a crossing point of the river Thames. He easily defeated two of Cunobelin's sons before heading for Camulodunum which soon surrendered or was captured. Roman control of southern Britain was quickly established, building on the compliance of native 'client kings' who were allowed to retain authority over their tribes in return for their practical and political support of Rome.

After AD 49, the Twentieth Legion marched out of Colchester as the frontiers of Rome's newest province were extended to the west and north. The military base at Colchester was converted to become a new 'colonia', a settlement for retired army veterans. Roman Colchester now had a 'Roman' population of very varied ethnic origins. More than half of the Roman army comprised auxiliaries, who came from every part of the empire, rather than legionaries, who were required to be Roman citizens.

With the new colony of Colchester barely established, a sudden terror threatened its very survival. The Iceni of Norfolk had been early allies of Rome, but when the kingdom was annexed following the death of Prasutagus, his widow, Boudica, led her people in rebellion. As the gathering British forces approached Colchester they were joined by the Trinovantes of Essex, whose motives were explained by the Roman historian, Tacitus: 'The [Roman] settlers drove the Trinovantes from their homes and land, and called them prisoners and slaves' (Tacitus *Annals*, xiv 31). When Boudica attacked with an estimated 120,000 followers, terrified residents barricaded themselves within the newly built temple of Claudius. Here they withstood attack for a reported two days, before the rampaging Britons forced their way into the temple, burning and killing. To this day, evidence of the total destruction by fire of the Romans' first capital at Colchester is visible whenever a town centre site is excavated.

The British revolt was ruthlessly suppressed, but not before the Roman towns at London and St Albans had been similarly destroyed by fire. It is hard to imagine how peaceful co-existence between Roman settlers and the surviving British population could easily be re-established. Colchester archaeologist Philip Crummy notes changes after AD 60 in pre-Roman sites around Colchester which had continued in use after the conquest. At Stanway, where the clearest evidence of collaboration between Britons and Romans has been found, burials in the cemetery ceased after the Boudican revolt. Meanwhile Sheepen, which had been a major commercial and industrial site both before and after the Roman conquest, 'changed radically in character from an industrial area to a sanctuary', with the subsequent building of four temples (Crummy, 1997, 86, 107).

Although the Trinovantes had been implicated and defeated in the Boudican revolt, there is substantial evidence that they survived as an organised community, though now lacking political autonomy, well into the Roman period. As the streets of Colchester were gradually cleared of rubble, former residents returned and new settlers arrived. New, modest town houses were built, although in the early decades these were fewer in number than those that had been burnt down. In addition, the nervous residents soon gained the belated protection of massive town walls.

Even within Colchester, the Roman population of the late 1st century probably remained small, and, as retired veterans took British wives, influences passed in both directions so that with each generation it became harder to distinguish one population group from another. Encouraging this new sense of unity in order to prevent future rebellion was the deliberate policy of Agricola, governor of Britain from AD 78-84. According to the biography written by his son-in-law, Tacitus:

'He [Agricola] wanted to accustom them [the Britons] to peace and leisure by providing delightful distractions. He gave personal encouragement and assistance to the building of temples, piazzas and town-houses, he gave the sons of the aristocracy a liberal education, they became eager to speak Latin effectively and the toga was everywhere to be seen' (Tacitus *Agricola* I 21).

Such policy could be observed in the later construction of a Roman temple and theatre at Gosbecks, site of the British capital of Camulodunum.

The British tribal elite around Camulodunum had been significantly Romanised even before the Roman invasion. Those who avoided involvement in the Boudican rebellion and retained their estates may have readily adopted the Latin language and begun building rural villas or rebuilding farmsteads to proclaim their new 'Roman' identity. However, Britons taken captive during the initial conquest or subsequent revolt were frequently sold as slaves. A tombstone in Tyne and Wear Museum mourns a Catuvellaunian slave, from Essex or Hertfordshire, who had married her Syrian master. The human dimension of this loving union between two races within Roman Britain is poignantly summed up in the tombstone's additional Aramaic inscription: 'Regina, freedwoman of Barates, alas'.

Whoever was buried beneath the Mersea Barrow, the mound itself must have been constructed by slaves or labourers, many probably of British descent, working under Roman or Romanised masters. But the choice of monument was made by a family or individual with status, wealth and a range of cultural influences. The selection of a barrow might have been influenced by pattern books deriving from mausolea such as that of Augustus in Rome, or from traditional burial practices brought by migrants from the Roman province of Belgic Gaul. It is most unlikely to have been the product of a joint enterprise between 'Britons' and 'Romans' living in separate communities on or close to Mersea Island. But the extent to which the builders of the monument were inspired by examples from Roman, British or other cultural traditions presents a complex and challenging question.

2   The date of the Mersea Barrow

New scientific methods such as carbon dating or dendrochronology have transformed the ability to date some archaeological finds. However, where such absolute dating is impossible due to the absence of organic material, alternative methods are used, based on the context of an artefact, such as the layer of material in which it was found in the ground or the style in which it was made. Often objects are found together, and the dating of one can provide a date for the whole group. Thus, Arthur Wright in 1912 compared the glass urn and lead box found inside the Mersea Barrow with others which showed similarities in design. The excavator, Samuel Hazzledine Warren, was happy to accept his suggestion of a late 1st century date, based on the dating of comparable finds known at the time.

The beautiful green glass urn found in the Mersea Barrow may have been specifically procured, or imported from the empire some years before it was used to contain the cremated remains. Glass urns were rarely used for this purpose until the later 1st century, when they become more common, especially in the south east of England. Robert Philpott, in *Burial Practices in Roman Britain* (1991, 26-7) notes: 'More certainly within the 2nd century are glass urns in wealthy burials at barrows in the south-east', citing 'Mersea Mount' as an example.

When Volume 3 of the *Victoria County History of Essex* was published in 1963, the article on 'Mersea Mount' was closely based on the 1913 excavation report. However, a new provisional date for the barrow, based on the pottery fragments, was slightly later than Warren's original conclusion. The locally made 'coarse black ware', now gave the 'impression of a date about AD 100-20'. This was probably because the writer, M R Hull, Curator of Colchester Museum for more than 25 years, had ample opportunity to study the collection again. His revision concurs with a note in the 1913 report that a glass urn similar to that found at Mersea had been discovered at Colchester together with two small jars of 'Durobrivian' ware, which could have been of early 2nd century date.

As well as physical remains such as artefacts or pottery sherds, other related burials can help to cast light on the significance and approximate date of the Mersea Barrow. Colchester has a late Iron Age tumulus (burial mound) as well as a wealth of Roman cremation burials, some identified by tombstones. On Mersea Island, several burials of the late Iron Age and early Roman period have been found, while further afield in Essex and beyond its borders, tumuli erected during the early Roman period can still be identified.

3   Comparative local burials

(a) Belgic cremation burial, Fairhaven Avenue, West Mersea

In the century before the Roman conquest, high-status 'Belgic' burials had taken place on the island. In 1979, four pottery vessels with cremated bone were unearthed by a householder in Fairhaven Avenue. Pottery expert Isobel Thompson described this burial as including 'an A:2 pedestal urn with a copy of a "Gallo-Belgic import", providing rare dating evidence' (Thompson, 1981, 63-5). This suggests that a Trinovantian family, probably farming an estate on Mersea, was in touch with influences from the continental provinces of the Roman Empire. There is no way of telling whether descendants of these pre-conquest inhabitants remained on their land after the invasion, but, if willing to accept the new regime, they probably became members of a newly Romanised population.

(b) The Lexden Tumulus and Lexden Mount, Colchester

First excavated in 1924 by Philip and Ted Laver, the Lexden Tumulus with its rich 'Belgic' burial probably dates from between 15-10 BC. In common with the Mersea Barrow, this now shallow mound contained the cremated remains of an important individual. However unlike that at Mersea, the tumulus was found to contain a rich array of damaged grave-goods, of which the most striking was a silver coin of the Emperor Augustus, mounted as a portrait medallion. The tumulus is now believed to be the grave of Addedomaros, a Trinovantian ruler at Camulodunum. The finds within the monument are clear evidence of the close relationship between local tribal rulers, the Roman province of Belgic Gaul and even the emperors of the rapidly expanding empire. (These diplomatic links probably date from around 54 BC when Julius Caesar, attempting the conquest of Britain, made treaties with both the Trinovantes and the Catuvellauni.)

The Lexden Mount, a separate burial mound excavated by the Morant Club in 1911, was disappointingly found to have been totally robbed-out, leaving only a few fragments of Roman tile and pottery. This suggests that it was closer in date to the Mersea Barrow than to the Lexden Tumulus.

(c) Roman 'brick tomb', West Mersea

Discovered in 1923 close to the villa site and wheel tomb described below, the cremated bones and teeth of a child aged 12-15 months were contained within a glass urn with a lead lid, which had retained slight textile impressions. As seen from the photograph (Fig 21), the urn was similar to that found in the Mersea Barrow, though smaller with a wider neck. It was placed within a *voussoir* (wedge shaped) flue tile, above which, standing on a flat tile and protected by another tile, was a small pottery lamp. This was stamped with the name 'IEGIDI', evidence that the lamp was made in Italy between AD 90-140 and thus dating the tomb to the 2nd century.

The items in this Mersea burial, which can be seen in Colchester Castle Museum, were contained within a square tomb-structure built of flat red bricks or tiles, surrounded by a mass of broken tile embedded in red mortar. This tomb was unfortunately destroyed during building work

Fig. 21 Cremation urn and lamp from the West Mersea 'brick tomb'

(d) 'Wheel tomb', West Mersea

This amazing discovery, close to Mersea's south shore, was first thought to be the foundation of a Roman lighthouse, and the adjacent lane is known to this day as 'Pharos Lane'. Excavation by the Essex Archaeological Society in 1897 revealed a structure sixty-five feet (*19.8 metres*) in diameter. At the centre was a small hexagonal chamber, from which six walls radiated to join a 3ft (*0.9 m*) thick encircling wall, before projecting another 4ft (*1.2 m*) beyond it, as external buttresses. Six additional buttresses occupied each space between these, making twelve in all, thus giving the structure the appearance of wheel spokes. The circular wall was built entirely of large tiles on foundations of ragstone and mortar, with no sign of a floor or doorway. No artefacts or burials were found within the structure, and, although drawings and photographs survive, remains of the structure have since been lost, despite its extremely rare archaeological significance.

Fig 22 The exposed foundations of the Mersea 'Wheel Tomb'

The closest surviving British parallel to this West Mersea site seems to be the foundation of a circular Roman tomb at Keston, near Bromley in Kent (for more information see *www.cka.moon-demon.co.uk/kestonvilla.htm*). The Keston example has no inner dividing walls, but a circular wall of 8.8 metres in diameter, with external buttresses, less than half the size of the Mersea 'wheel tomb'. Both examples were erected close to a Roman villa complex, with adjacent burials.

By comparison with the Keston circular tomb and similar structures in Italy and Germany, the Mersea wheel-tomb can be interpreted as the mausoleum of an important local individual, probably an occupant of the extensive Roman villa now largely beneath the nearby West Mersea church. The inspiration probably came from the mausoleum of Augustus, built in Rome for the imperial family in 28 BC. This circular stone building was covered by a tumulus, described by the Greek geographer, Strabo, as resembling a hill. A pillar projected through the mound to display a statue of Augustus, whose burial place was at its base. Interestingly, many roofing tiles and three pieces of dressed stone were found at West Mersea, indicating a possible roofed chamber. It is likely that the circular wall enclosed an earth mound, thus forming a tumulus above the tomb.

(e) The Bartlow Hills, Cambridgeshire (formerly Essex)

This was once reputedly the largest barrow group in Europe (see Fig 13), with seven enormous mounds dated to AD 80-140. Excavated during the early 19th century, the three largest surviving barrows yielded several examples of glass vessels containing cremated bone. Unlike the Mersea Barrow, however, there was also a rich array of grave goods, most of which were destroyed by fire in 1847, although three small items may today be seen in Saffron Walden Museum, Essex. Some of the burials were placed within wooden chests or a brick chamber, in some cases lit by iron lamps. Above these, the mounds were built up from layers of soil and chalk, the largest being nearly 50 ft (*15 m*) high.

Despite much scholarly discussion, little is known for certain about the purpose of such a vast, conspicuous barrow cemetery. A recent study by members of Reading University, *The Bartlow Hills in Context*, concluded in 2009:
> 'We argue that the barrows are actively and symbolically charged statements about power and identity. The most striking pattern to emerge from GIS [Geographic Information System] analysis is a focus on display to a local rather than a transient audience.'
(Eckardt *et al*, 2009, 47).

This suggestion of Roman tumuli as having territorial significance might equally be applied to the Mersea Barrow, constructed on the highest ground near the north shore of the island, and perhaps marking the boundary of the estate belonging to an important Roman villa.

4   Who built the Mersea Barrow?

In recent decades there has been considerable debate surrounding the origin of burial mounds, or tumuli, in the western parts of the Roman Empire. Those constructed in and around Rome itself may have been influenced by the round tumuli of the Etruscans in what is now Tuscany, developing into the 'great circular tombs with masonry and brick drums' or more modest 'cone-shaped mounds of earth and low retaining-walls of stone', several of which were built beside the Appian Way to the south of Rome (Toynbee, 1971, 179). Even on the western fringes of the empire, wealthy Romans sought to emulate the Mausoleum of Augustus. Toynbee suggests that for the unusual walled tumuli at Keston (Kent) and the West Mersea wheel-tomb, 'the provincial builders had at their disposal architectural sketch-books or manuals compiled in southern lands.' It should be noted that Warren believed that the Mersea Barrow had also been constructed by a professional mound-builder (1913 Report, 126).

The tumulus at Lexden is a rare example of a round barrow constructed in eastern England before the Roman invasion. Such monuments had not been built in Britain since the late Bronze Age, eight centuries previously, but would still have been evident in the landscape. Early scholars such as Warren believed that Romans did not build tumuli, but it is significant that use of this type of monument only returned to Britain in an area where British tribes had greatest contact with the Roman Empire. There are clear indications that the ruling elite at Camulodunum had diplomatic and trading contacts with Rome as well as close cultural connections with the Belgic peoples of Rome's western provinces. It is likely that the Lexden tumulus was influenced by contacts with the continent, rather than a harking-back to the earlier round barrows of the Bronze Age.

The Roman province of *Gallia Belgica,* or Belgic Gaul, conquered by Julius Caesar in 57 BC, is the location of a series of notable burial mounds in the area inhabited by the Tungrian tribe, now in modern Belgium. However, the earliest of these tumuli did not date from the pre-Roman period but 'seem to have appeared suddenly in the last quarter of the 1st century AD, because they have no clearly evident predecessors' (van den Hurk, 1986, 28). Van den Hurk observes that 'the same phenomenon is to be seen in all regions where concentrations of tumuli occur during the

Roman period, with the exception of Thracia.' Considering the reasons for this, he concludes that this form of burial mound was brought into the region by newcomers from the empire, presumably the 'Roman' builders of the new rural villas in these areas. It is probably significant that several tumuli were erected in Essex during the early period of the Roman occupation. Remains of Roman round barrows from the late 1st or 2nd centuries have been identified at Plumberow Mount near Hockley; near Langley, Uttlesford; at Little Shelford, Foulness; at South Ockendon Hall, Thurrock, as well as the outstanding example of the Mersea Barrow.

Once eastern England had been occupied by armies and civilians from different parts of the Roman Empire, the cultural practices of the incomers found a ready reception among those Britons who had already encountered the more sophisticated lifestyle of Romanised continental neighbours. By the mid-2nd century, large new Roman town houses had been built in Colchester, while in the countryside beyond, for example at Alresford, rural villas complete with mosaic floors and hypocaust (underfloor heating), were being built. Although these might have been built by Roman officials or estate owners, it is equally likely that they were built by Romanised British landowners, seeking to replace former timber buildings in the luxurious new style. Excavation of a villa at Little Oakley, near Harwich, has revealed a complex sequence in which a sunken floored structure on a site inhabited in the late Iron Age was succeeded in the later 1st century AD by a timber building, followed by a 'corridor villa' with masonry foundations built in the second half of the 2nd century AD.

The island of Mersea has always appeared to offer the ideal location for one or more Roman villas. The sheltered creeks, deep channels and sandy beach provide good harbour facilities, and there is some evidence of a Roman road leading from the mainland towards what later became known as King's Hard. Close to this favoured position on the south shore of the island, evidence has been found of what must have been either an extensive Roman villa or 'a collection of buildings concentrated on a small harbour' (Crummy, 1997, 71-2). The present West Mersea church, begun shortly before the Norman Conquest, contains a large quantity of Roman brick, clearly visible in the strengthened corners of the tower. And for several centuries, whenever a grave was dug in the churchyard, sections of mosaic or tessellated floor were frequently revealed. These supplied a convenient base on which to rest the coffin, before the churchyard became full and was closed around 1900, a new cemetery being provided in Barfield Road.

In 1730, a new garden was under construction at West Mersea Hall, adjacent to the church, and the Essex physician and antiquarian, Dr Cromwell Mortimer, was invited to inspect a Roman mosaic pavement uncovered by workmen (Fig 23). Digging additional test holes in the churchyard, he was able to establish much of the design, concluding that the floor measured 21 ½ ft (*6.5m*) by 18ft (*5.5m*). The design on the West Mersea mosaic pavement is very similar to one found on North Hill, Colchester, probably dating from the first half of the 2nd century. Over the years, further sections of Roman paving have been discovered, covering an area of 100 ft (*30m*) by 50 ft (*15m*). Part of a tessellated pavement was also discovered near St Peter's Well close by, suggesting that this was already a recognised water supply.

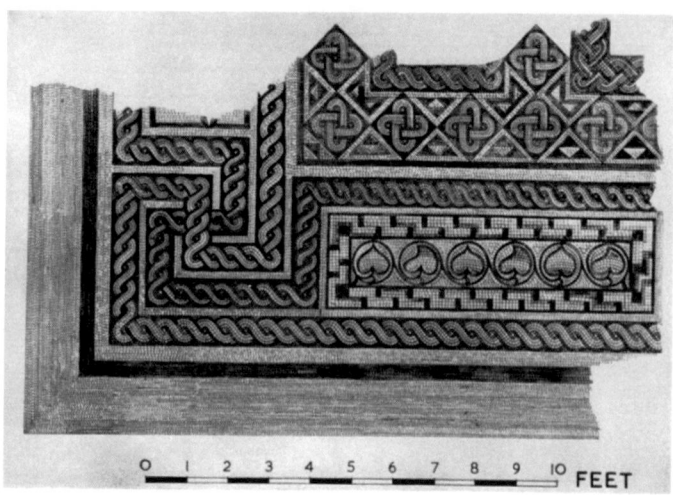

Fig. 23 Section of the mosaic pavement near West Mersea Church

Although the site of the West Mersea villa has been investigated on several occasions, a full excavation is obviously impossible and most of the artefacts discovered in the area over previous centuries have been lost. With its proximity to the brick tomb and wheel tomb described above, the villa seems to have been the home of a wealthy individual. If this was a 'Roman' incomer, he might have come from Gaul, or anywhere else in the empire, bringing pre-established ideas of fashionable elite burials. However, although the villa appears entirely Roman, this might have been the rebuilding of a farmstead or estate centre already existing during the late Iron Age on this favourable site. What might have begun as a smaller house could have been extended or rebuilt as the owners became more secure in their 'Roman' identity, prosperity and status.

The Mersea Barrow was probably constructed during the 2nd century, when Roman citizens and Romanised natives in the new province of Britannia were increasing in confidence and wealth. While the ethnic origin of the individual buried beneath the Mersea Barrow is unknown, the cinerary urn, lead casket and tile-built tomb are demonstrably Roman. What is more, all the diverse materials used to create the burial chamber and lead container might have come from the construction site of a Roman villa, built or extended at around the same time. As Ernest Black has pointed out in a recent, as yet unpublished, paper:
> 'Three different types of building stone were combined with broken *tegulae* and flat tiles, together with crushed tile (for *opus signinum* flooring), mortar and yellow ochre, used as a pigment in wall-painting ... It is as if the occupant of the tomb was being provided with the construction materials that were being used at the same time in building a new residence for the living, presumably other members of the same family.'

He goes on to consider the lead casket, formed of squares of lead cut from a larger sheet. Whereas many such burial containers would have been provided with a lid of the same material, or possibly a large tile, this was closed with material hitherto unused in the burial: two wooden boards. This may have been 'because oak fittings, perhaps including window-shutters and doors, were an important element in the new building for the living and so oak, like the other materials, was also regarded as due to the dead.' (Black, 2012, 1-2).

This relationship between building materials used in the Barrow burial chamber and in Roman villa construction provides strong evidence of a connection between the builders of the Barrow and the owner(s) of a nearby villa, who commissioned it as a tomb for one of their dead. Since the deceased occupant of the Barrow was obviously of high status, and the villa close to West Mersea church is known to have been extensive, it certainly appears likely that the two were connected. However, the Mersea Barrow is on the opposite shore of the island and a long way from the 'cemetery' area close to the West Mersea villa, which included the magnificent 'wheel tomb' and child's 'brick tomb'. The wheel tomb, covered by a substantial tumulus and perhaps surmounted by a monument as was the Mausoleum of Augustus, must have created a very visible landmark to ships using the River Blackwater, proclaiming to all who saw it the wealth and importance of the villa's occupier.

In an addendum to his paper, Ernest Black refers to a recent study of monumental tombs or tumuli in the territory of the Treveri, a Gallic tribe whose chief town was Trier, on the banks of the Moselle in Germany (Krier and Henrich, 2011). In fifteen examples all the tombs were built within one third of a mile of the associated villa. Most of these were also sited where they would offer an impressive spectacle when seen from a nearby road or waterway. This concern for visibility to travellers can be seen in other tumuli of south east England, such as the 'Six Hills' group of Roman barrows, built beside what became the Great North Road in Stevenage (Hertfordshire).

It is very likely that there were other Roman villas on Mersea Island, although evidence of these is elusive. The fabric of East Mersea church includes Roman brick, and in 1923, Dr Philip G. Laver reported to the AGM of the Essex Archaeological Society that a 'fine specimen of tesselated pavement' had been donated by Mr J King of East Mersea, to the Museum of the Colchester Philosophical Society (Laver, 1923, 5). The likelihood of a villa at East Mersea is strengthened by the discovery near Fen Farm in 1980 of a hoard of 657 Roman coins, buried by a wealthy resident during the troubled times of the 3rd century. Scattered coins and *tesserae* (small, square paving tiles) have also been recorded at various locations across the island, while fragments of Roman pottery were excavated in several of the West Mersea 'test pits' dug by Cambridge University's Higher Education Field Academy programme between 2006 and 2010. One site where a villa may very well have been built is within half a mile of the Mersea Barrow. A letter sent to the curator of Colchester

Museum in 1980 reported discoveries there of Roman material, including fragments of a tessellated pavement (Read, 1980).

The lie of the land suggests that the Mersea Barrow would not have been visible from the villa close to West Mersea church, about three miles away, and might not have been related to that villa. Perhaps, alternatively, the two tumuli of the Mersea Barrow and the West Mersea Wheel Tomb might have been a result of shared traditions or competing constructions by villa owners on the island's north and south shores. The fragments of tessellated pavement, possible evidence of a villa close to the Mersea Barrow, may be supported by topographical evidence. A nearby Iron Age 'red hill' at the edge of the saltmarsh north of the barrow continued in use during the Roman period, producing a regular supply of essential salt.

Before the Strood causeway was built in the late 7th century, travellers reaching Mersea by land might have used a ford across the Pyefleet Channel, noted by Warren as due north of the Mersea Barrow (1913 Report, 119). A villa near this location would also have been close to the likely Roman road to East Mersea. Thus, while the West Mersea villa was strategically placed on rising ground behind the harbour and beaches of the south shore, a villa on higher land near the north shore would have overlooked the landward route between Mersea and Colchester. Anyone arriving either by boat to the south shore, or by road and tidal ford to the island's north shore would have been greeted by a conspicuous funerary monument which also served as both landmark and power statement.

The existence or otherwise of a Roman villa in the vicinity of the Mersea Barrow may never be proved. If there were one, it is a more likely candidate for the residence of the individual commemorated by the building of the Mersea Barrow. However, if this were not the case, the whole western half of the island was probably attached to the West Mersea villa. Its owners might have chosen to mark both the northern and southern limits of their estate with conspicuous funerary monuments. Thus, whether travellers arrived on Mersea by land, sea or river, none could doubt the significance and high status of the dominant local family.

5   Burial rituals

It has always been accepted that the burial chamber and funerary containers within the Mersea Barrow are of Roman origin. However, there is far more speculation about the origin of the tumulus constructed above the burial chamber. When Warren excavated the Mersea Barrow in 1912, he found unexplained features in the construction of the mound. It had been carefully built up of different distinct layers: compact grey material, comprising earthy quartz sand, and 'incoherent gravel and sand'. There were deposits of charcoal, calcined bone and broken shell mixed with charcoal, which Warren attributed to 'cooking sites'. The most mysterious feature was an unexplained 'red stratum', deliberately mixed out of crushed red tile, mortar and yellow ochre. This had been spread over the entire surface of the sealed tile tomb and for some distance around it. A layer of charcoal covered the red stratum above the tomb, and, above this, several more red layers alternated with the material of the mound. Warren suspected that these layers 'may have been connected with some custom which was observed at the ceremony of interment' (1913 Report, 128).

Recent work on late Iron Age burial practices has identified contrasting traditions among the tribal elite of eastern and south-east England. Rosalind Niblett has compared the rich grave-goods of 'Welwyn-type', burials, with another tradition exemplified by cremation burials at Stanway and Lexden, both near Colchester, and Folly Lane, St Albans. She observes:
> 'Neither at Folly Lane or Stanway did the burial signal the end of ritual activities ... At Lexden, Folly Lane and (probably) Stanway, mounds were constructed over the destroyed mortuary pits and it is possible that ... these became foci of commemorative rites' (Niblett 2003, 35).

At both Lexden and Stanway, it seems that grave goods and feasting vessels accompanying the cremated bodies had been ritually destroyed. Although Lexden predates the Roman invasion, the Stanway cemetery remained in use until the Boudican revolt, and may demonstrate a continuity of burial rites which survived the Romanisation of the tribal elites. The Stanway cemetery comprised four adjacent ditched enclosures, three of which were in use after the Roman invasion. Each enclosure had been built around a wood-planked mortuary chamber where there was evidence of ritual destruction of grave goods: 'Unfortunately, only a small proportion of the objects found their way into the backfilled remains of the chambers'. Plates and drinking vessels had also been smashed, implying that the enclosures 'were special places for the performance of processes and rituals associated with death and the disposal of the dead' (Crummy, 1997, 26). In contrast, several secondary burials within the enclosures retained an impressive and undamaged array of grave goods, particularly that of the 'doctor' with his surgical instruments and gaming board.

In his 2012 paper, Ernest Black considers these anomalous deposits within the Mersea tumulus in the light of both the Stanway cemetery and an early 3rd century Roman barrow at Holborough Knob, Kent, excavated in the 1950s. Here, the deceased had been buried in a pit surrounded at ground level by a rectangular wooden structure which had then been destroyed. The pit had been sealed by a mound of puddled chalk which was then covered with turf, in its turn spread over with a deposit of burnt material including wood, nails and molten glass. Finally, a barrow had been constructed over the burial. It was clear that an elaborate sequence of funerary rites had taken place, which included smashing amphorae (storage jars) and pouring over this debris a libation of unidentified liquid. Black suggests that these rituals might have some parallel in the mysterious layers of the 'red stratum' and deposits of charcoal, broken pottery and crushed shells which Warren observed in the Mersea barrow. (The 'libation of unidentified liquid' at Holborough may also be compared with the resinous substances identified in 2013 with the cremated bone from the Mersea Barrow - see page 72.)

It is difficult to guess at the nature of the rituals which accompanied the burial of cremated remains at the sites discussed above. Noting within the Mersea Barrow the quantity of shells, including one example of scallop, as well as bricquetage (debris from salt-making) brought from the nearby shore, Black explores pagan attitudes towards marine symbols of 'the interface uniting human activity with the sphere of the divine.' Whatever the beliefs of the native tribes, it is clear that the pre-Christian Roman Empire encompassed a great variety of funeral practices which 'did not differ essentially from those they found among many of the populations of north-western Europe' (van den Hurk, 1986, 27).

In his excavation report, Warren expressed puzzlement about the purpose of the remarkable 'red stratum', sealing and covering the tile-built tomb beneath the Mersea Barrow, which he could only attribute to 'some custom which was observed at the ceremony of interment' (1913 Report, 128). Black notes reports of a similar red material in association with Roman burials of this period. A red coating of crushed tile and mortar had been painted on the retaining wall of the circular Roman tomb at Keston (Kent), a smaller though similar structure to the Mersea wheel-tomb. Even more conclusively, the brick tomb containing a child's cremation at West Mersea was 'surrounded by a circular mass of broken tile embedded in red mortar' (Benton, 1924, 129). The use of this red coating, of no practical use in burial, must, as Warren suspected, derive from some ritual funerary observance which as yet we cannot fully understand. However, it was not, as Warren imagined, a tradition peculiar to 'primitive' tribes, but was a practice employed by Romans in eastern Britain to embellish their most sophisticated tombs.

6 Further investigation

(a) Archaeological material from the mound

In the century following its excavation, the Mersea Barrow has become better known and understood as a significant tumulus (burial mound) of the early Roman period. Sadly, however, it also suffered periods of neglect and unrestricted access, allowing the illicit removal of the remains of the tile-built tomb structure which Warren had hoped could be reconstructed and further studied. When in 1912 the lead casket, glass urn and cremated bone were taken to Colchester Museum for public display, it was fortunate that Warren had also taken careful measures to preserve samples of archaeological, botanical and geological material from the barrow and the ground on which it had been built.

The pottery fragments photographed by Warren and published in his 1913 Report as Plates F and G, 'Minor Relics' (see page 17), were among the archaeological material which he had carefully collected from the excavated mound and sent to Colchester Museum. At the request of Ernest Black, this material was located in 2012 by Steve Yates of Colchester and Ipswich Museum Service. During that year and the early part of 2013 it was re-examined by Stephen Benfield of Colchester Archaeological Trust, who 'spot dated' 58 potsherds. His observations are discussed in the paper 'The West Roman Mersea Barrow (Mersea Mount)' by Stephen Benfield and Ernest Black, due to be published in *The Transactions of the Essex Society for Archaeology and History,* Volume 4 (Fourth series), 2014 (forthcoming). The two authors kindly allowed advanced sight of this paper, which explores many significant aspects of the Mersea Barrow. Some observations regarding the date of the barrow have been briefly summarized in the following paragraphs.

Among the material from the mound, Benfield identified a number of small, undecorated sherds of hand-made pottery. Some, tempered with crushed burnt flint, may have dated from the Late Bronze Age or Early Iron Age, while other, sand-tempered sherds were typical of pottery of the Middle Iron Age [c 350-50 BC]. These fragments of earlier occupation may well have been deliberately included in the earth and gravel brought to the site by the barrow's builders. They were distributed in the grey material at the core of the mound as well as in the lower levels of gravel above. In contrast, Benfield observed that the broken Roman pottery was distributed throughout the core of the mound but not in the layer of gravel.

The Roman potsherds identified by Benfield were dominated by small-to-medium fragments of grey ware, one of the most common types of Roman pottery. Some of these were slightly abraded, indicating that the broken edges had been worn down before their inclusion in the mound. Several had come from beakers, bowls or jars and platters, probably produced around Colchester during the late 1st-early 2nd century. However, there were also several medium sized sherds from the lower wall of a large grey ware jar, some of which could be fitted together (Warren's Plate F, nos 5 and 6, see page 17). These were found near the base of the barrow mound, suggesting that the pot was broken around the time that the barrow was under construction. The pieces are decorated with a 'chevron' design, angled groups of lines forming an open lattice pattern, and appear to have been burnished with 'a possible black surface finish'. The burnished lattice decoration of this jar, the only one represented by more than one or two sherds, can be seen on jars from Colchester classified as form CAM 278, dating from the reign of Hadrian (AD 117-138) to the mid-3rd century.

In his *Discussion* of the Roman pottery, Benfield observes that most of the sherds which he examined indicate that 'as an assemblage the pottery dates to the late 1st-early 2nd century'. This concurs with the dating suggested by M R Hull (VCH Essex III 1963, 160), rather than Warren's assumption of a late 1st century date for the construction of the Mersea Barrow. However, Benfield pays particular attention to the group of chevron decorated grey ware sherds, 'most firmly associated with the construction of the mound', which appeared to have come from a vessel of form Cam 278: 'If so, the nature of the burnished pattern in relation to this particular form could indicate a vessel of Antonine (or slightly later date) rather than Hadrianic date. This suggests that the Mersea barrow mound was most probably constructed in the late Hadrianic-Antonine period'. (The Antonine emperors ruled from AD 138-192). This later dating of the barrow, as perhaps constructed around the mid 2nd century or slightly later, is supported by the authors' observation of a fragment of roof tile 'recovered by Warren from disturbed soil near the eastern side of the mound ... [which] has a thickness of 17-20mm, suggesting a date after *c.* AD 150'.

The elaborate rituals which accompanied the construction of the barrow (as discussed on pages 64-66 above) may be indicated by the different materials incorporated within the mound. As described by Warren in his 1913 Report, these included deposits of broken oyster shells, charcoal and fragments of calcined bone (later confirmed as animal bone) which the excavator had interpreted as the remains of cooking hearths. There were also numerous fragments of briquetage from coastal Red Hills, prehistoric and early Roman pottery, and worked flint flakes. In their forthcoming paper, Benfield and Black observe that not only the hearths, but also the diverse material incorporated into the core of the mound, may have represented significant aspects of the mound's construction and dedication:

> 'If the grey material was chosen for the core of the mound both because it contained cultural material relating to the ancestors of the dead person as well as for its location between the cultivated world of men and the untamed world of the gods, this was reinforced by the hearths with their broken fragments of oyster shells.' (Benfield and Black, 2014, forthcoming)

(b) Botanical specimens

Warren's carefully gathered botanical specimens and seeds have experienced several relocations since their initial inspection by Clement Reid in 1912. They were initially deposited in the Essex Museum of Natural History at Stratford, later to become the Passmore Edwards Museum. After this closed in 1998, its library and natural history collection were put into storage by the Essex Field Club, who in early 2012 moved their collections into new premises at Wat Tyler Country Park, near Pitsea, Essex. Unfortunately, those collections which include the material originally deposited by Warren are not yet available for further investigation, and it has only been possible to refer to the observations made a century ago.

The list of Warren's botanical specimens as identified by Reid was reconsidered in late 2011 by Jerry Bowdrey, Senior Curator of Natural History at Colchester and Ipswich Museum Service. He questioned Reid's observation that this was an assemblage of plants 'growing on wet meadow land', suggesting that, although this was a limited list from which to draw firm conclusions, it indicated a more well-drained soil. The list included one species of cultivated plant ('Good King Henry': *Chenopodium bonus-henrica*, once a common kitchen crop but now rarely found). Two species came from a more general habitat; six favoured lighter soils and two favoured wet soils. Most species identified are still found in north-east Essex although Betony (*Stachys officinalis*) and Corn Spurrey (*Spergula arvensis*) are becoming rare. It is hoped that at some time in the future the seeds will once again become accessible for expert scrutiny, allowing further information to be discovered about the natural environment of Mersea Island at the time when the Roman barrow was built.

(c) Analysis of the cremated bone

The mystery at the heart of the Mersea Barrow which most frequently engaged visitors gazing at the glass cremation urn on temporary display in Mersea Museum was the simple query: 'Whose bones were these?' When a substantial grant from the Association for Roman Archaeology was added to generous donations from islanders and visitors during 2012, it appeared that some kind of answer might at last be in prospect. At the end of January 2013, the bones were removed from their urn in Colchester Museum, carefully packed up by Steve Yates and delivered by courier to the laboratories of Wessex Archaeology at Salisbury, for analysis by Senior Osteoarchaeologist, Jacqueline McKinley. Her final report, including an appendix by Rhea Brettell of the University of Bradford, is due for publication in *The Transactions of the Essex Society for Archaeology and History,* Volume 4 (Fourth series), 2014 (forthcoming). Some significant and unique discoveries made during the painstaking process of analysis are summarized below.

Despite an eager desire to know the geographic or ethnic origins of the individual buried beneath the Mersea Barrow, there was no expectation of obtaining this information from cremated remains. Early analysis identified a male aged between 35 and 45, most of whose remains appeared 'relatively large and robust, with some marked muscle attachments, particularly in the lower limb'. He was 'regularly engaged in strenuous walking/running', and signs of soft tissue injury suggest he may have suffered a tear in one of the major thigh muscles. More surprisingly, evidence from spinal lesions and new, excessive bony growths indicated that he suffered from Diffuse Idiopathic Skeletal Hyperostosis [DISH], a joint disease which today is found mainly in men over fifty. Jacqueline McKinley reported that she knew of no other cases of DISH recorded in cremated remains.

The weight of cremated bone retrieved from the funeral pyre for burial beneath the Mersea Barrow was 1730.5 grams, 'among the highest from any cremation burial, of any period, in the British Isles'. The remains were in good condition, with around 70% identifiable to specific skeletal elements. However, although the urn was only partly filled, some skeletal elements were missing which could not have been totally consumed by the fire. Smaller bones from the hands and feet may have been left behind among the pyre debris, but the urn also contained far fewer fragments from the arms and ribs than from the legs. It is not clear what happened to the remains left out of the urn. In 1912 the excavator, Warren, searched unsuccessfully for the site of the funeral pyre, and it is indeed possible that other human remains left at the pyre site are still concealed beneath the unexcavated, western half of the Mersea Barrow. It is also possible, speculates Jacqueline McKinley, that some bones such as those of the hands may have been distributed as mementoes for the deceased's relatives or friends.

Before the analysis could be completed, an unexpected problem arose. The bones were found to be coated with a strange, sticky substance which could not easily be rinsed off. To make matters worse, when attempts were made to scrape it away, it emitted a choking smell and unpleasant dust which resulted in Jacqueline McKinley having to work in mask and gloves for the first time ever. There was an urgent need to identify the ancient material, which appeared to be some kind of resin. A specialist team, led by Professor Carl Heron of the University of Bradford, was found to be researching just such organic matter in archaeological contexts. Even more fortunately, a research student, Rhea Brettell, was currently working on a PhD thesis exploring the 'identification of resinous materials in Roman mortuary contexts in Britain and evaluation of their significance'. Samples of the Mersea material were sent immediately to Bradford for molecular analysis, and the results were to prove of major archaeological significance, not limited to Britain.

In a detailed report supported by 32 pages of scientific data, Rhea Brettell concluded that the mysterious coating on the bones from the Mersea Barrow consisted of a mixture of two different resinous substances. This identification was 'the first chemical confirmation for the use of resins in a Roman cremation burial'. The first type of resin had come from the widespread sub-family Pinaceae which includes cedars, larches and pines, with the latter 'believed to have special significance in Roman mortuary beliefs'. Even more significant was the larger quantity of a different type of gum-resin, produced by trees of the genus Boswellia, and widely known as frankincense. This has a characteristic chemical composition which gives it a unique fragrance as the most highly valued incense in the ancient world.

There are many references in classical texts to the use of frankincense and other perfumes or unguents at various stages of the funeral rites. Rhea Brettell quotes one of the Roman poet Martial's epigrams urging 'Shameless Zoilus' to empty his pockets of 'the half-cremated frankincense you took from the pyre'. Such precious ointments were frequently used to anoint bodies before burial, but it is extremely rare for any archaeological evidence to survive. Although a report of 1834 suggests that a substance resembling frankincense was detected with high quality grave goods within the Bartlow Hills, this evidence had been destroyed, along with most of the finds from the site, in a disastrous fire. Before the analysis of the Mersea remains, frankincense had been identified at only four other archaeological sites worldwide: in Egypt, Nubia and Yemen.

Because the resins had survived so well in the Mersea cremation urn, it was clear that they had not been used to accelerate or quench the funeral pyre, or to anoint the body before cremation, but must have been applied in some form to the cooled bones. It is possible that some of the pine resin found with the bones may have provided a seal to close the open mouth of the glass urn, but the frankincense must surely have been added to the bones as a liquid or unguent prior to their burial. Unfortunately, there are no directly comparable examples to help in the interpretation of this discovery. Neither do we know how the frankincense was imported, probably from east Africa, into Britain. Yet for some as yet unknown reason it became part of the funerary rites for one important individual, based not at the major Roman city of Colchester but on the coastal outpost of Mersea Island, an island unrecorded in any known Roman account.

When Samuel Hazzledine Warren excavated the Mersea Barrow in 1912, he was puzzled by the identification of yellow ochre mixed with crushed red tile which he considered 'may have been connected with some custom which was observed at the ceremony of interment'. If so, that was just one feature of the elaborate ritual which accompanied the departure of Mersea's dead Roman from this world into the next. His cremated bones had already received a libation of extremely rare, valuable and probably sacred frankincense. Jacqueline McKinley observes that the unexpected and currently unique discovery of this substance 'has enriched our comprehension of the wealth and magnificence of this individual's funeral rites and his reflected social status and connections'. This significant individual, whose remains lay concealed for nearly two millennia, has been brought into the daylight, and some secrets of his medical condition and elaborate funeral have finally been revealed. Whether born in Britain, or anywhere in the farthest reaches of the Roman Empire, his physical condition suggests that he might have served in the Roman army (and perhaps been invalided out). However he arrived on Mersea Island, he obviously held a major social, possibly familial and probably administrative position in this corner of Roman Britain.

7   Conclusion

During the probable heyday of Roman Mersea, three impressive tombs are known to have been constructed in the western half of the island: the 'wheel tomb' (see page 56); the 'brick tomb' (page 55) and the Mersea Barrow. All can be dated to the 2nd century AD when Roman Colchester, although no longer the capital of the province of Britannia, was a major centre of cultural life and official administration. They may have been commissioned by one or possibly two elite landowning families living in a newly built coastal villa, whose antecedents may have originated in the area or migrated since the Roman invasion. In the absence of a written record and until further archaeological evidence becomes available, we can only speculate as to who was buried within each tomb and why the different tomb-structures were adopted. Even less is at present known about the elaborate funeral rites which accompanied each interment.

Although on first consideration the tombs seem very different, they share sufficient similarities to be linked to the same cultural group. Both the Mersea Barrow and the child's brick tomb contained cremations in a glass bowl, concealed within some form of casket inside a tile or brick structure. Both the Mersea Barrow and the wheel tomb were probably influenced by the famous Mausoleum of the Emperor Augustus, with its earth mound above a masonry burial chamber. All three tombs were devoid of grave-goods, suggesting Roman rather than British burial traditions. However, two showed evidence of some form of ritual associated with a symbolic red coating, while the third, the wheel tomb, is linked to the same ritual by its association with the Keston circular tomb. The rituals observed in the construction of the Mersea Barrow, which caused its first excavator to regard the tumulus as British rather than Roman, can be seen as a significant feature of burial rites in use during the 2nd century by a predominantly 'Roman' population of south east Britain.

In the decades leading up to the Roman conquest, West Mersea was no remote backwater, but a fertile, productive settlement on the shores of a busy waterway, within easy reach of the British capital at Camulodum with its close contacts with the Roman Empire. When the legions arrived, native inhabitants may have fled or been driven out: more likely their leaders submitted, co-operated with newly arrived Roman administrators and gradually adopted their language and lifestyle. Certainly, there was likely to be intermarriage with British women. In the century that followed, at least one wealthy, cultured individual ordered the building or conversion of a substantial villa on the island's sheltered southern shore. Whether originating from Britain, Gaul, or any other part of the empire, the villa's 'Roman' inhabitants enjoyed all the luxuries which expert craftsmanship and distant trade could supply. They also spared no expense in providing elaborate tombs for their dead. Their burial rites included rituals which might have been passed down from tribal forebears or adapted from the descendants of such local families, but which remained a significant part of their ceremonies for the dead before the coming of Christianity.

Regrettably, Mersea Island has now lost two of its rare and important Roman tombs. The third and most conspicuous, Mersea Barrow, has survived in the rural surroundings of Barrow Hill farm, only threatened in 1929 when the site was advertised for sale as 'suitable for development as a building estate'. The tumulus may originally have been constructed to make a statement, visible for miles around, about the power and territorial control of the individual or family who commissioned it nearly two thousand years ago. Today it still makes a powerful statement, reminding us of islanders of another age, mourning their dead and seeking their permanent commemoration. Mersea Barrow provides a potent, physical link with our Roman precursors of nearly two millennia ago. With continuing care and skilful conservation it will continue to be an enduring symbol to islanders and visitors alike, for many centuries to come.

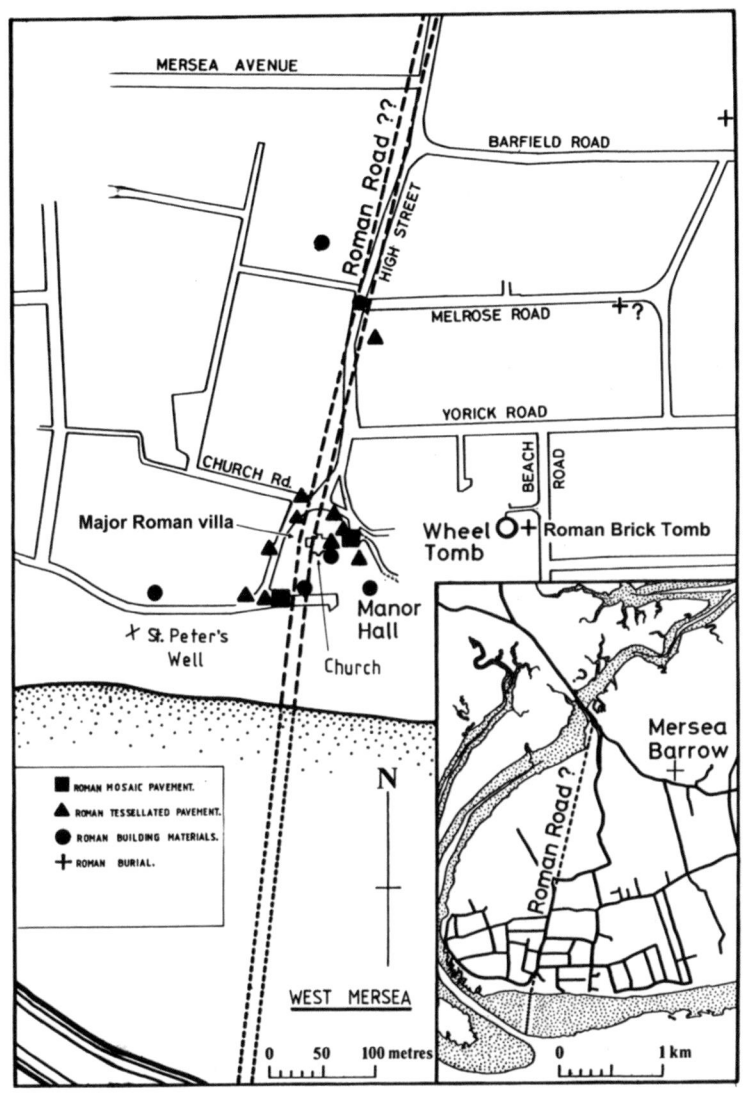

Fig. 24 Plan of probable Roman sites at West Mersea

Bibliography

Books, reports and periodicals

Baring-Gould, Sabine, *Mehalah: a story of the salt marshes*, first published 1880

Benton, GM, 'Roman Burial Group discovered at West Mersea', *Transactions of the Essex Archaeological Society*, new series Vol 17, Part 2, 1924, pp 128-130

Black, EW, 'Romano-British burial customs', *Archaeological Journal* Vol 143, 1986, pp 201-39

Clarke, David TD & Davies, G Mark R, *Roman Colchester*, Colchester Archaeological Trust, 1979

Conley, Joseph F, *Reflections: Musings of an Old Missionary*, 2009

Crummy, Philip, *City of Victory*, Colchester Archaeological Trust, 1997

Cunnington, M E, 'Bronze Age Barrows on Arn Hill, Warminster' *Wiltshire Archaeological Magazine*, 1912 pp 539-41

Dunnett, Rosalind, *The Trinovantes*, 1975

Eckardt, H, Clarke, AS, Hay, S, Macaulay, S, Ryan, P, Thornley, DM and Timby, J, 'The Bartlow Hills in context: report on recent excavations', *Proceedings of the Cambridge Antiquarian Society*, Vol 97, 2009, pp 47-64

Fox Davies, AC (ed), *Armorial families: a directory of gentlemen of coat-armour*, Vol 2, 5th edition 1929

Goddard, AR, 'The Bartlow Hills', *Transactions of the Essex Archaeological Society*, ns Vol 7, 1899, pp 349-55

Haines, Leslie B, 'The neglected Mersea Island Barrow', *Essex Countryside*, 1969

Holloway, Ben, 'An archaeological evaluation at 20 Yorick Road, West Mersea, Essex', *Colchester Archaeological Trust Report* 255, Jan 2004

Holloway, Ben, 'An archaeological watching brief at 20 Yorick Road, West Mersea, Essex', *Colchester Archaeological Trust Report* 330, July 2005.

Hull, MR 'Roman Essex' in Powell, W R (ed), *Victoria County History of Essex* Vol 3, 1963, pp 157-161

Krier, J and Henrich, P, 'Monumental funerary structures of the 1st to the 3rd centuries in the area of the Treveri' in Raymans, N and Derks, T, *Villa Landscapes in the Roman North*, (Amsterdam, 2011)

Laver, Dr Philip G, FSA, 'Paper Read to the Society on 26 April 1923 [Notes on Mersea Island]', reprinted from *Transactions of the Essex Archaeological Society*, Vol 16, part 4

McKinley, Jacqueline, 'The Analysis of cremated bone' in *Human Osteology in Archaeology and Forensic Science*, by Cox M and Mays, S, 2000, pp 403-412

Niblett, Rosalind, 'The Native Elite and their Funeral Practices from the 1st century BC to Nero' in Todd, Malcolm (ed), *A Companion to Roman Britain*, 2003 pp 30-41

Oakley, Kenneth P, 'The Life and Work of Samuel Hazzledine Warren, FGS', *Essex Naturalist* Vol 30, 1959, pp 143-61

Orr, K, *An Archaeological Excavation at Handford Place (formerly Handford House)*, Colchester Archaeological Trust Report 323, 2005

Philpott, Robert, *Burial Practices in Roman Britain*, 1991

Rodwell, Warwick, 'Historic churches - a wasting asset', *CBA Research Report* Number 19, 1975

Saunders, H, 'Prehistoric and Roman Settlement in Essex', *East Anglian Archaeology* 136, 2011, Essex County Council, p 81

Thompson, Isobel, 'A "Belgic" Cremation Burial Found at West Mersea', *Essex Archaeology and History*, Vol 13, 1981, pp 63-5

Toynbee, JMC, *Death and Burial in the Roman World*, 1971,

Van den Hurk, LJAM, *The Tumuli from the Roman Period of Esch, Province of North Brabant*, 1986

Warren, S Hazzledine FGS, 'The opening of the Romano-British Barrow on Mersea Island, Essex', Morant Club, (reprinted from *Transactions of the Essex Archaeological Society*, ns Vol 13, 1913, pp 116-40)

Warren, S Hazzledine, 'Report on certain Botanical and Geological observations made during the opening of the Romano-British Barrow on Mersea Island'*Essex Naturalist* Vol 17, 1912, pp 261-5

'Report of Excursion to Mersea Island (the 427th meeting)' *Essex Naturalist* Vol 17, 1912, pp 229-34

'Mersea Mount' Planning Application Information Statement, Inkpen Downie Architecture and Design, August 2006

Unpublished papers

Benfield, Stephen and Black, Ernest, *The West Mersea Barrow, Mersea Mount*, 2013

Black, Ernest W, *The West Mersea Barrow, Mersea Mount*, 2011, revised Jan 2012

Bowdrey, J, *Current status in north-east Essex of plants identified by Clement Reid from Mersea Barrow land surface (from Tarpey and Heath, 1990)*, Jan 2012

Brettell, Rhea, *Analysis of organic matter from a cremation urn, Mersea Island* (Archaeological Sciences, University of Bradford) 2013

Correspondence between S Hazzledine Warren and A G Wright, 1912-13, (Colchester Museum Archives)

Documents and photographs relating to the Mersea Barrow (Colchester Museum Archives)

Documents and photographs relating to the Mersea Barrow (Mersea Island Museum archives)

Read, J W M unpublished letter dated 28.8.1980 to 'Mr Clarke' (Mersea Island Museum archives)

McKinley, Jacqueline, *Mersea Island Barrow, Essex, Cremated Bone Publication Report* (Wessex Archaeology) May 2013

Internet websites
(consulted November 2011 - April 2012 and August 2013)

http://books.google.com/advanced_book_search (Google books on line)

http://cka.moon-demon.co.uk/kestonpage.htm (Council for Kentish Archaeology: Keston tombs)

http://en.wikipedia.org (Wikipedia on line encyclopedia)

http://hansard.millbanksystems.com/commons/1958/jun/24/barrow-hill-west-mersea-tumulus (Question in parliament regarding Mersea Barrow)

http://list.english-heritage.org.uk/results.aspx (English Heritage list entry, Mersea Mount)

http://unlockingessex.essexcc.gov.uk (Essex County Council Archaeology [SEAX] website)

http://www.Ancestry.co.uk (Family history)

http://www.arch.cam.ac.uk/aca/westmersea.html (Cambridge University Higher Education Field Academies: Reports from West Mersea)
http://www.camulos.com (Archaeology and history of Colchester)
http://www.cat.essex.ac.uk/all-reports.html (Colchester Archaeological Trust reports)
http://www.colchester.gov.uk/article/1687/Viewing-a-Planning-application (Planning applications to Colchester Borough Council)
http://www.eafa.org.uk/catalogue/4832 (East Anglian Film Archive 'On Camera', Mersea Island)
http://www.essexcountystandard.co.uk/archive/ (Essex County Standard online archive)
http://www.essexfieldclub.org.uk/portal/p/Archive+Search (Essex Field Club archives, especially *Essex Naturalist*)
http://www.gazette-news.co.uk/archive/ (Colchester Gazette online archive)
http://www.merseamuseum.org.uk (Mersea Museum website)
http://www.oxforddnb.com (Oxford Dictionary of National Biography on line)
http://www.roman-britain.org (Roman Britain website)

Illustrations and picture credits

Unless listed otherwise, all images are courtesy of Mersea Island Museum.

Front cover: The entrance to Mersea Barrow (Pat Kirby)
Back cover: Mersea Barrow in the Snow (Len, Michael and Andrew Harvey, 1987, by permission of Mrs R Harvey)

Fig. 1 Samuel Hazzledine Warren at "Sherwood", Loughton, in October 1931 taken by Professor K. Absolon. (*Essex Naturalist*. Vol. 30. Plate 9 p. 144), reproduced by permission of Essex Field Club
Fig. 2 Warren's photograph of Mersea Barrow from the west
Fig. 3 Warren's plan of the Mersea Barrow

Fig. 4   *Arthur Wright (Curator) and Dr Henry Laver (Honorary Curator)*
   (Colchester and Ipswich Museum Service)
Fig. 5   *Wright's 1912 photograph of the lead casket and glass urn*
Fig. 6   *Warren's photographs of some 'Minor Relics' from the mound*
Fig. 7   *Warren's cross-section of the barrow*
Fig. 8   *Warren's 'Section of the Tomb: Conjectural Restoration'*
Fig. 9   *Roman roofing tiles* (Wikimedia Commons
   http://en.wikipedia.org/wiki/File:Tiles_Fishbourne.JPG)
Fig. 10   *Warren's flashlight photograph of the opened tomb*
Fig. 11   *Hammond postcard of the open excavation trench*
   (Colchester and Ipswich Museum Service)
Fig. 12   *The Excavation Report (cover of Morant Club reprint), 1913*
Fig. 13   *The Bartlow Hills, print of an 18th century engraving*
Fig. 14   *Early postcard of Barrow Hall (Barrow Hill Farm)*
Fig. 15   *1929 Sale Map of the Barrow Hill Estate, showing the Mersea Barrow in the bottom right corner.*
Fig. 16   *Mersea Barrow, grazed by chickens, in 1966.* (Essex County Standard)
Fig. 17   *Mersea Barrow in 1969, following clearance and renovation* (Leslie B Haines, by permission of Mrs K Haines)
Fig. 18   *Burial Mound Handover* (Essex County Standard, 16 April 1975)
Fig. 19   *Visitors to Mersea Barrow on 17 February 2012* (Sue Howlett)
Fig. 20   *Colchester Museum employees moving the Roman cremation urn into its temporary display cabinet in Mersea Museum* (Pat Kirby)
Fig. 21   *Urn and lamp from 'Brick Tomb' near West Mersea Church*
   (Colchester and Ipswich Museum Service)
Fig. 22   *Early photograph of the exposed foundations of the West Mersea Wheel Tomb*
Fig. 23   *Section of the mosaic pavement near West Mersea Church,*
   (Victoria County History Vol. 3. (Oxford University Press, 1963) p.158, by permission of the Executive Editor)
Fig. 24   *Map of probable Roman sites at West Mersea* (Karbacz, Elsie M, A Short History of Mersea, 1980, plan revised by Tony Millatt, 2012)